Good Old Times

Rev. Elijah Kellogg

A reprinting on the occasion
of Gorham, Maine's 250th anniversary
with a new foreword by State Historian
Robert M. York

New England History Press
in collaboration with
Gorham's 250th Anniversary Committee

Good Old Times was originally published in
1878 by Lee and Shepard Co., Boston.
There were subsequent printings of which this
is a copy of the 1905 edition. It is published
December, 1985 as a cooperative project
by the 250th Anniversary Committee of
Gorham, Maine 04038, and the New England
History Press of Somersworth, New Hampshire
03878.

Library of Congress Catalog Card Number: 85-62658
International Standard Book Number: 0-89725-060-5

DEDICATION

As a representative of the six living great-grandchildren of Elijah Kellogg, I wish to express our thanks to Gorham's 250th Anniversary Committee for republishing *Good Old Times.*

Of course, I don't remember my great-grandfather, Elijah Kellogg, but I heard many stories about him from his grandson, my father Laurence Kellogg Batchelder.

As children, my sister (Mary Batchelder Hackett) and I spent many pleasant hours visiting our cousins Sheila, Nancy, and Mary Noyce Kellogg at the Old Kellogg Place. We visited the "Marrying Tree" (an old apple tree where many people held their weddings), played in Granpa Kellogg's old carriage, and roamed the fields and beach, where his boat called a "pinkie" was stored. This boat can be seen at the Mystic Seaport, Mystic, Connecticut.

I also remember going to many "Elijah Kellogg Days" at the Kellogg Church in Harpswell. Professor Wilmot B. Mitchell, author of *Elijah Kellogg the Man and His Work*, was generally one of the speakers. It was always an interesting day.

The town of Gorham was Elijah Kellogg's "second home," and I know he would be happy to have *Good Old Times* a part of the 250th Anniversary celebration.

Gorham, Maine   BETSY BATCHELDER CLOUGH
August 1985

FOREWORD

The Gorham 250th Anniversary Committee is to be congratulated for returning *Good Old Times,* a classic account of pioneering days in Gorham, Maine, to print. This new edition should afford those interested in heritage and history the same pleasure that readers of earlier generations found in the book's stories of life on the raw cutting edge of the Maine frontier in pre-Revolutionary War days.

Written by the Reverend Elijah Kellogg, Jr., *Good Old Times* repeats the tales Kellogg heard as a young lad from family and friends when visiting or living in Gorham. He was a great-grandson of Hugh and Elizabeth McClellan, Scotch-Irish immigrants who, after brief stops in Boston, York, Wells, and Falmouth, arrived in Gorham in 1738-39 as the second-settled family of Narragansett No. 7. Their experiences were typical of the era and place—wolves, bears, foxes, beaver and other wild animals in abundance; Indians, usually friendly but sometimes hostile; the French and Indian War, seven years spent living in the fort on the hill; poor harvests and near-starvation with only hazelnuts, boiled beech leaves, and lily roots for food; rich harvests of corn and venison aplenty; spruce gum, maple sap; oxen; masting; "burns"—the nuts and bolts of frontier living.

Born May 20, 1813, Elijah Kellogg, Jr., was the son of the Reverend Elijah Kellogg, pastor of the renowned

Second Parish (Orthodox Congregational) Church of Portland, and Eunice McClellan of Portland, the granddaughter of Gorham's Hugh and Elizabeth.

He was a very keen, lively, restless lad who occasionally skipped church to swim in Back Cove. At the age of thirteen he went to sea; three years later he turned his hand to working on a family farm in Gorham. This direct knowledge of both the sailor's and the farmer's life, gained through his own experiences, and through the stories he heard from those he met along the way, served him well when he came to preach and later to write. While at Gorham, he enrolled in its academy, and at age twenty-three he entered Bowdoin College, graduating in 1840. Now determined to follow in his father's footsteps, he attended Andover Seminary; after ordination he became pastor of the Congregational church at Harpswell—adjacent to Brunswick—where he served till 1856. For the next decade he labored in Boston with the Mariner's Church and Sailor's Home. Though he summered in Maine, the years from 1865 to 1882 were spent mostly in Boston, working as a writer and supply pastor. In 1882 he returned to Harpswell to live and again served the Congregational church there, except for several years in Topsham, until his death in 1901. The church to this day is known as the Kellogg Church.

Save for two declamations, "Spartacus to the Gladiators" and "Regulus to the Carthaginians," Kellogg did almost no writing till the age of fifty. *Good Old Times* was his first book, and always his most popular. Most of his books—altogether he wrote twenty-nine—are similarly set in Maine locales that were intimately known to him: the Elm Island series depicts life along the coast near his Harpswell parish, the Whispering Pines series, life at Bowdoin College.

A moral purpose was evident in all of Kellogg's work, for he continually sought to promote the virtues of integrity, hard work, self-sacrifice, and courage. However, he did not lard his writings to the point of turning off his main audience—young men. That he was effective in making himself heard by them was evidenced by the popularity of his books and the numerous testimonials he received. He remains to this day Harpswell's best-known and most-beloved citizen and one of Maine's leading writers of boys' books. Gorham, too, is proud of him, for though his account of the town's early days was fictionalized, he was truly its first historian. On the occasion of Gorham's 150th birthday in 1886 Kellogg was honored by being named the principal speaker of the celebration. It is very fitting that one hundred years later the citizens of Gorham should be given the opportunity to hear him speak again through this new edition of *Good Old Times.*

Orr's Island, Maine   Robert M. York
September 1985   Professor Emeritus of History, USM
and State Historian

GRANDFATHER'S HOMESTEAD.   Page 10.

GOOD OLD TIMES;

OR,

GRANDFATHER'S

STRUGGLES FOR A HOMESTEAD.

BY

REV. ELIJAH KELLOGG,

AUTHOR OF "ELM ISLAND STORIES," "PLEASANT COVE STORIES,"
"WHISPERING PINE STORIES," "FOREST GLEN STORIES,"
ETC., ETC.

BOSTON:
LOTHROP, LEE & SHEPARD CO.

PREFACE.

——◦◦◦——

THE characters described in this story are real, the names given are the names they bore, and their very language is often quoted. With one exception, the houses in which they spent their later days are still standing, and their numerous posterity are scattered through the States.

With little aid from external circumstances, they fought their way from poverty to affluence, manifesting a heroism in which there was no trace of ferocity, and a piety unsullied by bigotry.

Neither the severity of the climate, the stubbornness of the soil, nor the barbarity of the savage, could force them to abandon the land upon which their feet were planted.

5

Representing, as they do, to a greater or less extent, the character of a large portion of the settlers of these New England States, the history of their struggle commends itself to all. May those who aspire to make the most of themselves revere the virtues and emulate the resolution of those who broke the path for their descendants, and rendered the culture of the present age possible.

CONTENTS.

CHAPTER VIII.

CHAPTER IX.

CHAPTER X.

CHAPTER XI.

CHAPTER XII.

GOOD OLD TIMES;

OR,

GRANDFATHER'S STRUGGLE FOR A HOME.

CHAPTER I.

WHAT GRANNIE TOLD ME.

THERE is no subject more worthy the attention of their children than the stern virtues and sterling worth and piety of the men who laid the foundations of the institutions which we enjoy, and our appreciation of which we have vindicated in the recent terrific struggle, thus reconsecrating the manhood of our institutions by the same baptism of blood with which their infancy was sanctified.

As the struggle recorded in the following pages is not fiction, but fact, we beg leave to introduce our readers at once to the principal person from whom we derive our information.

In the town of Gorham, Maine, is a fertile farm of about two hundred acres, skirted by a small stream called Little River, and sometimes Warren's

9

River.   The farm lies at the roots of high hills that
slope gradually to the stream, and is now occupied
by Major William Warren, one of the few persons
in his neighborhood who retain the lands possessed
by their forefathers.   The house, which is of two
stories, built when there was a rage for two-story
houses in Maine, and which replaced the log camps
of the first settlers, is situated upon a gentle elevation a few rods from the bank of the river.   In the
kitchen, which occupies nearly the whole length of
the house, is the old panelling of the walls, and
there too are the ancient dressers which once glit-
tered with their long rows of pewter dishes, now
replaced by commonplace crockery.   In the centre
of the side of the room is one of the real old-fash-
ioned fireplaces, with the oven between the jambs,
and a chimney up whose capacious throat you can
look and see the stars.   In the right-hand corner is
the dye-pot, and a couple of blocks upon which the
children sit and nestle together in the cold winter
nights.

    The old house faced to the south, and the out-
buildings, running to the east and at right angles
with it, formed a sheltered and sunny door-yard,
which was occupied by an enormous pile of wood,
composed of sections of the trunks of large trees,
fifteen feet in length, mixed with the largest branches, the smaller brush not being worth hauling home
in that day.

    It is the afternoon of a bright, sunshiny day in

February; the snow is falling from the roof, and the ice dropping from the glazed logs of the wood-pile; near to which is a youth just entering upon manhood, who evidently considers it to be the chief end of man to chop wood. Stripped as to his outer garments to the waist, his arms bare to the elbows, the perspiration dropping from his face, he is junking up a hemlock log into four-foot cuts. He is getting ready the night's wood, both for grandmother's room and the old kitchen fireplace, — for grandmother always has a fire built in her room to go to bed by. While he is thus engaged, a woman, aged, but vigorous and straight as a rush, comes out from the house and fills her apron with the great chips he is cutting out.

" A cold spring," she observes, looking up at the bright sun.

" Why, how can you tell that, Grandma'am ? " inquires the boy.

" Because, child,

> ' As far as the sun shines in on Candlemas day,
> So far will the snow blow in before May,' —

and to-day is Candlemas."

This is Grannie, — the youngest child of the family of which we are to speak. Her maiden name was Martha McLellan; that by marriage, Warren; and she is now about seventy years of age.

Being gifted with a retentive memory, she was in possession of all the traditions of her family, en-

riched by her own experience as the wife of a pioneer and the mother of a lusty family reared in
hardship.   She was rather small of stature, but of a
frame uniting great strength and endurance, dark-
complexioned, and with a keen black eye, which,
when she was roused (for Grannie had a temper of
her own), would flash like a snake's.   " I know I
am quick — God mend me ! " she would sometimes
say, by way of apology ; " but if soon up, I'm soon
down.   It's the old Highland temper.   And what's
the good of a pewter axe ? "

But if Grannie had *grit*, she had grace too, and a
noble spirit of her own, — God bless her !   She was
hospitable in the highest degree, and so kind and
good in sickness that she was sent for from far and
near, — better than half the doctors, — for she knew
all the herbs of the mountains.   Inheriting an iron
constitution hardened by a life of toil, her only in-
firmities were occasional attacks of a rebellious
colic, which, however, generally yielded to persist-
ent applications of hot water and pumpkin-seeds.

There were few books in the house.   Neighbors
were distant, and in the long winter evenings,
before a blazing fire, a dish of apples between the
andirons (such as *were* andirons, made to hold up
an eight-foot fore-stick, with hooks on the back for
the spit), the apples flanked by a pitcher of cider,
— O, was not our Grannie then a real treasure ?
She was not our own grandmother, you must know,
but our grandmother's sister ; yet we always called

her Grannie, and she was just as good. Didn't she knit our mittens, and knit the name into them too? Didn't she come out into the field to bring us a luncheon when, in her opinion, we had eaten too slight a breakfast? and didn't she worry and make all the house worry when we were out late in the woods? Hadn't we a right to call her Grannie?

The Major's wife we used to call Aunt, though she was but a second-cousin's wife. But didn't she bake for us in the old oven such three-cornered biscuit and turnovers and pan-dowdies, and roast raccoons, and have such glorious fires to welcome us when we came home wet, cold, and hungry from the woods!

But to the point. The great incentive to this eager preparation of the night's wood was a desire to propitiate Grannie, whom he had offended and touched in a very tender spot. It was this that made the chips fly and the perspiration run. She generally wound up her stories about hauling masts for the king's ships by saying, " Well, they used to have a barrel of rum at father's, a barrel at brother Billy's, and a barrel at Cary's; and the barrel at our house they got more masts with, and it lasted longer, than the one at Billy's or Cary's."

Upon which we suggested that perhaps they watered it to make it hold out.

" Watered, is it! " she exclaimed, with an expression of scorn upon her features which would have done honor to Mrs. Siddons. " They were never

guilty of such meanness in those days. They had
no occasion, for they could drink their liquor and
carry it off, and thank God for it like honest men,
and not get drunk on a thimbleful as they do now.
They were not, to be sure, so full of compliments,
and stuck-up ways, and great pretensions to religion
and doing God's work by the job, as they are now.
But they had religion enough to keep them warm
in His house without stoves; and when they got
there, didn't sit fussing with their shawls, and
flaunting their ribbons, and picking themselves like
a hen in the sun. But they looked at the servant
of God, and heard what he said, and practised it
afterwards. They didn't backbite and talk about
their neighbors, but loved them and lived together
like brothers. Nobody ever thought of such a thing
as charging a neighbor for cattle to plough, or a
horse to go to mill, or a little seed-corn to sow. If
one was sick or poor, the rest helped him. They
put in his planting, or they cut his hay, or hauled
up his winter's wood, and looked for their pay in
the approbation of their own consciences, and of
Him who has said, ' Thou shalt love thy neighbor
as thyself.' Water spirit for hard-working men to
drink, indeed ! ''

Then, without deigning to wait for a word of
apology or explanation, she took her pipe, thrust
her thumb into the bowl to put it out, folded up
her knitting-work, and went to her room, though
it wanted a quarter of seven ; and for two long
months there were no more stories.

How we missed our customary evening feast!
We played "fox and geese"; we caught rats in
a meeting-house trap, and had a tame woodchuck,
we played "pull-up" with the neighbors' boys, —
which consisted in sitting down on the floor and
putting our feet one against the other, then taking
hold of an axe-handle and seeing which could pull
the other up. We even aspired to tell stories ourselves out of spite; but they sounded too flat, and
moreover we had to encounter Grannie's glances
of contempt, as we thus lamed ourselves "treading
in the steps of Cæsar." We shrewdly suspected
that Grannie herself was in somewhat the same pre-
dicament; for, like most old people, she was fond
of talking about the events of her youth, and liked
an attentive audience. But as to her yielding, — at
any rate until we were sufficiently punished and
penitent, — it was altogether out of the question.
Driven to desperation, we had on this day resolved
to do our best endeavor to melt her obdurate will.

There were three things that Grannie dearly
loved, — good tobacco, a rousing fire, and a cup of
green tea. About the middle of the afternoon we
presented her with a fig of nice tobacco, which we
had travelled six miles in the snow the night before
to get; and we had previously bunched onions in
the evenings for Captain Codman in order to obtain
money to pay for that, and for some little things
that boys need. This was well received and gave
us a ray of hope. The next stage of the process

was to prevail upon Aunt to give Grannie a cup
of tea that would "bear a flat-iron," to which she
readily agreed. It was a regular conspiracy. The
final stage was the great fire that Grannie loved.
All old people, as the circulation gets low in their
veins, love warmth. But Grannie was peculiar in
this respect. She loved to see the blaze and listen
to the crackling of the fire, if it was midsummer.
As the great majority of our readers never saw an
old-time fire, and never will, we propose to describe
the process of making it. First came the log, —
a green hemlock, four feet long and three feet
through, calculated to last two days. This was
either hauled into the house on a hand-sled, or
" walked in," that is, set up on end and worked
along, one corner at a time. It was rolled into the
fireplace upon two large sticks to keep it up from
the coals, and with half a bushel of snow on it.
Then came a back-stick two thirds as large on the
top, then a fore-stick eight feet long and a foot
through; then the brands and coals of the old fire,
surmounted with great clefts of rock-maple, oak,
birch, or beech, stark green, mixed with dry pine
and pitch knots. Finally a little blowing, by waving
a hemlock broom back and forth a few times (Grannie used to fan with her apron), and the whole mass
burst into a blaze, that went roaring up the chimney, and made the whole room as light as day.
There was no call for patent excelsior fire-kind-
lings in those days, when there were a bushel of

red-hot coals, a charred log, and the brands of the old fore-stick to begin with in the morning.

We are now, supper being ended and the fire having burned down to reasonable dimensions, all seated around the hospitable hearth. In the right-hand corner is Grannie; on the block between her knees and the jambs sits the penitent offender against the majesty of antiquity; on her left the grand-children and Aunt; in the rear of the group sits the Major, his handkerchief flung over his face in order to conceal any signs and sounds of merriment from the quick eyes and ears of his parent, watching the progress of the plot.

Grannie was evidently in a favorable mood. She had praised the tea, praised the tobacco, expressed her satisfaction with the fire. As she thus sat with her checked apron smoothed over her knees, — for though she had a silk gown for "dress up," and a string of gold beads, she would have scorned to wear anything for every day that was "boughten stuff" (not made at home), — her knitting-work lay in her lap, and she drew long and gentle whiffs through her pipe. It was plain that things were working, — that she was not, as usual, about to retire when she had finished her pipe, but had brought her knitting, and meant to spend the evening with us. Emboldened by these pacific signs, the youth observes, with a wink to Aunt, " I don't see how the old people ever got through with so much work. I am sure women nowadays couldn't begin to do it."

2

This was touching Grannie in a weak point. The
Major's wife was an early riser, — up with the crows.
Her cows always stepped over the pasture bars very
soon after sunrise ; while Grannie, with all her vigor
and faculty for turning off work, was never a very
early riser. She took it upon herself to reply.

"It was because they *worked ;* mother always said
that she never got her property by getting up early,
or sitting up late, but by working after she was up.
Sally here is a smart woman, smart as any of the
women nowadays; so is my darter, Betsy Libby.
But I wonder what they'd think if they had to milk
seven cows, and get breakfast for eight men, fill up
tubs and troughs with water to keep the clearing
fires from burning the camp up, and then get on to
the stallion, with a child before them, and ride
through the spotted trees down to mother's, and help
her spin, and then back to get dinner. I wonder
what they would think of that ! "

"They couldn't do it, Grandma'am," cried the
youth, his hands clenched, and his face red with
excitement and admiration. "It ain't in 'em."

"No, child," replied Grannie, "it ain't in 'em; it
never was in 'em, and it never will be in 'em. God
fits every back to its burden, and we were fitted for
ours. At any rate they were heavy enough, I am
sure of that."

"Now, Grandma'am, tell us about the time you
made Sam's trousers."

"Well, in those days there were no carding-mills

to card cotton and wool, nor cotton-factories to spin and weave, but everything we wore had to be made by hand. Sam was warned to go to general muster, and he had to have white trousers. There was a pair in the house that his father had trained in, and that he lotted upon wearing. We had to make things last in those days, and they were made to last: they wa'n't made to sell; but when he came to try them on after dinner, the day before muster, they were so old and threadbare they all came to pieces. There was a time! one o'clock the day before muster, and no trousers. My girls wa'n't married then, — smart girls they were, too, brought up to work. Though I say it myself, I could drive things then. 'Girls,' I said, ' we must weave the cloth, and make those trousers by morning.' ' O mother, it's impossible!' 'Don't tell me that, Betsy! Get the wheel, get the cards! Sam, clap the saddle on the mare and ride down to mother's and borrow her cotton-cards and some cotton-wool, for I'm jealous we haven't enough in the house.' We sat up all night, and never stopped to eat, only we kept the teapot between the andirons. I drew the piece in the loom, and wove just enough for the trousers, cut it out, and made 'em that night, and the next morning he wore 'em to training. That's the way we did things in those days."

"Now, Grandma'am, tell us about Uncle Billy, and the old Highland folks, and the Douglasses, clear from the bottom, clear from the roots, Grandma'am, do!"

"Not the Douglasses, child, — they were no kin to us; there was an old feud between us and the Douglass."

A celebrated French chemist, in his researches for a process to preserve wood from decay, cut asunder a small tree, and, placing it in a vessel filled with a red liquid, found that the liquid was drawn up by capillary attraction, even to the extremity of the branches and the very fibres of the leaves. Thus, as I sat in the chimney-corner, my chin on her knees, my eyes fixed on her face, and my mouth wide open, did the ancient dame impregnate my boyish fancy with the traditions of other days.

But of all the forms she summoned from the buried past, none ever made such abiding, loving, reverential impression as Uncle Billy, — the name by which he was known and loved far and near. To us the day dawned, and the sun rose and set, in Uncle Billy; he overshadowed us like a great presence. To be as tough, as resolute as Uncle Billy, was to us the sum total of life and life's happiness. Were cold, hunger, tempest, to be endured, we thought how would he have grappled with it. He was, according to Grannie, all that a friend should love or an enemy fear; and to her definition we gave a cordial assent.

There was a forest where we used to go and fell trees, by weeks together, in the short gloomy days of November, — a sombre and lonesome place, far from home. In the midst of it stood an enormous gray maple, green with the moss of many centuries, impossible to approach; for from beneath its roots came out a spring which, choked by dead leaves, windfalls, and withered branches, created all around it a quaking bog, which would not have borne a woodchuck, and would have ingulfed an army. How we did ache to cut that tree, just to see it fall! We should like to do it now. But since we could not fell it, we christened it Uncle Billy.

Often, as night drew on, as the shadows lengthened in the forest, and no sound was heard but the low creak of some swaying branch and the mournful sough of the wind among the pines, did we steal timorous glances at the old tree, and, as its form grew dim in the twilight, we almost expected to see the bark open, and the tall form and grave features of our stalwart ancestor emerge from it. As we resumed our clothes, and flinging the axe over our shoulder, set out for home in the twilight, we perchance mistook the echo of our own footsteps for those of some one following, and quickened our pace to the travelled road.

And here, before listening to our relative's narration in respect to the origin and fortunes of her family in the Old World, let us glance at the places where, notwithstanding all the disadvantages of ignorance, poverty, and war, they, with indomitable courage and trust in God, fought and conquered in life's battle.

As the traveller passes up the road leading from

Scarborough to the village of Gorham, at the distance of a mile from it he ascends a slight elevation, and his eye rests upon a row of locust-trees, by the side of a straggling wall, and an aged pomegranate, to whose withered branches a few green leaves, like friendship in misfortune, still cling. Near by is the remnant of an extensive orchard, the trees of which are decaying, — some hollow and prostrate, others surrounded by a wilderness of sprouts, striving with their green foliage to conceal the hoary parent, and to prolong its life. A lilac and a few currant-bushes covered with moss struggle for existence near to the cellar of what was evidently, at some time long past, a spacious house. The land around is desolate and forbidding, fast relapsing to the original forest; while the mind, upon contemplating it, experiences a feeling of regret at seeing savage Nature again resuming its sway where it is evident the hand of man has wrought, and human affections have taken root.

Ask any man past middle age, a native whom you may chance to meet, whose place that was or is, and he will tell you, "That was the 'Uncle Billy' place;" and almost any boy will tell you the same from traditional knowledge. Interrogate the aged man further, and he will tell you that these brown and barren fields once groaned with abundant harvests; the branches of those decaying trees once bent beneath the weight of choice fruit; large herds fed in the pastures; twenty cows filled the brimming pails; while upon that grass-grown cellar stood a noble house, and in it lived a man from whose hospitable door none ever went hungry away ; and he will probably wind up by telling you that they never had any town's poor in Gorham as long as Uncle Billy lived.   Thus the whole community seem to have assumed the task of keeping green the memory of a man who loved his country and his kind, but who had no son to keep his name in remembrance.

At the distance of a quarter of a mile from the principal village of Gorham, in the same direction, and just below what is known as the Academy Hill, near the banks of a brook, — now a mere thread, but which at the date of this story was a smart stream when fed from the full springs of the primeval forest, and which furnished to the pioneers many a dish of speckled trout, — stands a quaint-looking house of two stories.   The walls to the second story are of brick, — the ends and roof of wood.   The progress of improvement has replaced the old gable by a modern sharp roof, and some slight alterations have been made inside ; the great fireplace has given way to a stove ; otherwise the old house stands as the founders left it.

A few rods from it, and a little nearer the brook, is the site of the log-house in which those founders lived when not in garrison during the French and Indian wars, and from which they removed to the brick one, where, as we shall see, Elizabeth nursed the wounded savages.   Just below, a spring pours its water into a wooden trough, for the convenience of the traveller. To this spring, on the evening of the 18th April, 1746, Uncle Billy, then a boy, went to bring the night's water, while Indians ambushed the path on each side, and could have touched him with their hands. Upon the opposite side of the road, a few decaying apple-trees mark the spot where once stood the original camp in which the emigrants passed their first night.

In this house, built in 1773, the first brick building erected in Maine, the bricks of which were made by his own hands and those of his children, lived and died Hugh McLellan, and Elizabeth his wife, — the father and mother of Uncle Billy and eight other children, the youngest of whom, Martha, was our Grannie, to whom you have already been introduced, and who was, it is said, the very image of her mother. The story of their struggle I tell you as it was told to me, through many long winter evenings, at Grannie's knees, till I was afraid to go to bed lest I should meet an Indian in his war-paint on the stairs, and covered my head in agony in the blankets if a door creaked, or a nail, loosened by the frost, snapped among the shingles.

They were called in that day Scotch-Irish. Not that there was any admixture of blood, but a long residence in Ireland had given rise to the name. In the year 1608, by reason of the rebellion of the native chieftains in the north of Ireland, and their subsequent defeat and banishment, about five hundred thousand acres accrued to the crown, — that is, became the property of the king of England. These lands James I. settled to a great extent with emigrants from England and Scotland. Ireland had for ages been the back door to England and Scotland, through which the French had thrown forces into the kingdom, and aided the cause of insurrection. Therefore, as a bulwark against future aggressions, James determined to drive out the native Catholic Irish, and to replace them largely by a Protestant population of Scotch and English, but principally Scotch, — rough-handed and warlike, — whose lands were to be given them in fee-simple on certain conditions, and who might be safely counted upon to defend their property to the death. Thus being actuated by the strongest principles that operate upon the human mind, — self-interest, religious enthusiasm, and the antipathies of race, — it was supposed they would form a loyal population, that might prove a permanent bulwark against foreign aggression and domestic treason. As this was a pet measure of the monarch's, peculiar privileges were accorded them. Free schools were endowed, a university established, the extent of possessions limited, and all proprietors were compelled to reside on and cultivate their lands. Thus these Scotch emigrants obtained the name of Scotch-Irish, though, except in occasional instances, without any mixture of blood. Indeed, it was the great object of the king to prevent this, as it was upon the mutual antipathies of the two races that he relied for the success of his scheme.

Provision was therefore made that they should be
settled in different parts of the territory, it having
been found by a similar experiment in the time of
Elizabeth, that, instead of the industrious settlers
civilizing the wild Irish, the latter only envied the
superior advantages of their neighbors, and by means
of free access to their houses took occasion to steal
their goods and plot against their lives. The wild
Irish were therefore planted in the most level, open,
fertile part of the country, and on the lands that
were the most easily worked, in order that the superior quality of the soil might counterbalance the disadvantages arising from their natural indolence and
want of knowledge of agriculture. Thus also they
were exposed to the constant inspection of their
neighbors, and it was hoped that, from being mere
vagabonds, wandering from place to place with their
cattle, they might be gradually habituated to agriculture and the mechanic arts. To the others were
assigned the hills and the places of greatest strength
and command, and those of the most danger, — the
woods and wild parts of the country, — Ireland being covered — before they were destroyed to smelt
iron — with vast forests, the remains of which are
to this day found in the bogs. The old Irish were
also forbidden to drive their cattle from place to
place, or go " creaghing " as it was called, but compelled to a settled habitation and tillage. Each
landed proprietor was also required within a speci-
fied time to place a certain number of tenants on his

place. The cottages were also required to be built in the English style.

From this race sprang Hugh McLellan of Gorham, and Bryce of Portland, the ancestors of all of that name in Maine. They were a hard-handed race, who knew right well how to wield the claymore, and belonged to the order of saints who hewed Agag in pieces before the Lord, and who inscribed upon the muzzles of their cannon, " Lord, open thou my lips, and my mouth shall show forth thy praise." Their paternal ancestor, Sir Hugh of the clan Argyle, came into Ulster after the expatriation of the old Irish from the neighborhood. He received an allotment of fifteen hundred acres, according to the conditions of tenure, with the understanding that he was to render knight's service to the crown, and with his good sword hold his goods and lands against all comers, which he was nothing loath to do, being bred to arms from his youth. With the progress of refinement, the growth of knowledge, and of a more kindly and rational piety, his posterity became an industrious, God-fearing, manly race, who, losing the fiercer traits of their forefathers, retained their hardihood and strength of limb.

Let us, turning back the leaves of the years, imagine ourselves in the County of Antrim, in the Province of Ulster, in 1733, when the resolute Presbyterian, forsaking country and kin, with his young wife dared the privation of a strange land and a savage wilderness, stimulated by no romantic hopes of finding treasure or amassing a fortune, but that he might obtain that which was denied him in his native land, — a heritage for himself and his children, — and might escape those persecutions to which all who at that time differed from the Established Church were exposed, — a period in our narrative which will more properly form the subject of another chapter.

CHAPTER II.

NOTHING VENTURE, NOTHING HAVE.

IT is the end of October, but Old Ireland's fields
are green ; for, though the landscape is destitute
of forests, and the hedges which impart such an air
of beauty to the soil of England are replaced by
stone walls and ditches, — notwithstanding all this,
the exceeding greenness of the entire turf makes large
amends.   Nothing more quickly arrests the eye of
the traveller than the striking difference in the character of the dwellings and the methods of cultivation
that meet his view, especially when taken in con-
nection with the singular fact, that the most fertile
portions of the soil present the poorest dwellings and
the most meagre crops, while upon the steep and
stony hillsides, the cold, broken, and less fertile
lands, both the tenements and the crops are of a far
superior quality.   In those portions inhabited by the
Irish are fields which have been cropped with oats
and planted with potatoes, till the soil is so exhausted
that it will bear no longer, when it is left to itself to
spring up in weeds, briers, and nettles.   Heaps of

earth serve for fences, with a furze-bush stuck in a
gap for a gate. Some of these cabins are made by
merely building up three mud walls against the bank
of a ditch, laying on some poles for a roof, and covering them with sods and potato-tops, and look for all
the world like an overgrown dunghill. But the
cottages of the English and Scotch offer a strong
contrast. Most of them are built of wood or stone,
but even when constructed of earth, as many of
them are, present a very different appearance. These
are formed by setting four posts in the ground at
the corners, a frame for the door, and others for
windows. Around this frame the walls are built
with clay and chopped straw, two feet thick. Instead of a hole in the roof to let out the smoke, as
in the Irish cabins, there is a stone or brick chimney,
and the roof is well thatched with straw, and tight.
There is always a little spot enclosed for a garden,
and often bees in straw hives. The pigs and cattle,
though permitted to run about the door in the day-
time, are confined in their hovels at night. In all
the cottages of the Scotch quarter may be heard the
hum of the wheel, and the stroke of the weaver's
beam, while linen, yarn, and webs of cloth of all
degrees of whiteness contrast pleasantly with the
emerald hue of the turf.

It was past the middle of the afternoon of a Saturday, when a young man of apparently twenty-three
years, with a carpenter's axe flung over his shoulder, evidently returning from his week's work, and

good-humoredly exchanging greetings with those he met, or who sat smoking at their cottage doors, might be seen ascending an abrupt elevation, commanding a large extent of territory occupied entirely by Scotch. Its summit was crowned with a fortress of massive stone, rough from the quarry, and though without any pretensions to architectural beauty or ornament, of vast strength, the walls being seven feet in thickness. The house was built upon the edge of a cliff jutting into a bog, at the base of which flowed a brook of dark-colored water, which by a circuitous path reached the river Bann. Being built to the very edge of the little promontory, it was thus naturally impregnable on two sides. The narrow slits in the walls had been evidently loopholes for musketry, while in the larger apertures that served for windows were the stumps of iron gratings long since rusted off. From the front proceeded two angles which were also loopholed, and commanded the principal entrance, the door of which was of oak studded with iron bolts. In the original plan of the house, the whole ground-floor had been devoted to the storage of provisions and the reception of cattle in case of siege, while the upper story was the residence of the family and garrison, and was reached by a flight of steps formed by the projecting stones of the walls. The lower part, or keep, had been lighted only by loopholes, while the upper rooms were airy, and had large windows, which had once been grated, and were still fitted with strong oaken

shutters, studded, like the door, with iron. In
addition to this was an extensive court-yard, surrounded by a wall of great height and thickness,
enclosing the hovels of the cattle, and a fine spring,
which welled out from the side of the hill, and whose
surplus water, pouring through a narrow and grated
aperture in the wall, ran down the sides of the de-
clivity to the bog beneath. All along the course of
this rill, which, owing to the steepness of the descent,
ran with considerable force, were several little dams
made by children in their play, and at the lower
dam, which was made of stones and turf, much more
capacious than the others, and in the construction
of which they had evidently been aided by older
hands, was a sluice-way of wood, in which was a little
water-wheel, whirling with great velocity. Around
this were assembled a group of children, who, with
their legs bare to the knees, waded into the pond,
filled up the sluice with turf till the wheel stopped,
and then, suddenly pulling it away, set up a great
shout, and clapped their hands in glee, as the wheel
began to turn faster than ever.

The young man to whom we have referred had
now nearly gained the summit of the hill, and was
fast approaching the house. This was Hugh
McLellan, the son of Hugh, the present occupant
of the estate. Under ordinary circumstances, as he
was naturally light-hearted, he would have been
whistling a lively tune to beguile the road as he
returned from his labor ; for he was a ship-carpenter,

THE WATER WHEEL. Page 32

and had been all the week at work in a neighboring seaport. His father having given him his time at nineteen, he had by industry and prudence been gradually saving a little, and had been married nearly two years to Elizabeth McLellan. Her parents having died when she was a child, she had been adopted by a wealthy uncle, who, having escaped the misfortunes which befell the other branches of his family, had retained the broad lands of his forefathers. Though of the same name, they were but very distantly, if at all, related. Her uncle, offended that she had married a poor man and a mechanic, disinherited her. But Elizabeth, with a nobler pride, instead of sighing over her trials and making herself miserable by dwelling upon her past prosperity, set herself to learn all kinds of domestic work, that she might fit herself to be a helpmeet to the poor man she had married because she loved him, and, going into the family with Hugh's parents, — for her uncle had turned her out of doors, — excelled in a short time every member of the family in the very labors to which they had been always accustomed, but which were new to her. Impelled by her strong affection for her husband and offspring, there was no drudgery she could not cheerfully undertake and carry through.

"I may, as they tell me," said Elizabeth, with equal good sense and piety, "have married below my degree, a poor man, but I have married the man I loved, and that loves me, and that has the prop-

3

erty in himself, — one that is a God-fearing man and
dutiful to his parents. There is a promise to such,
and I have no fear but we shall get along."

Elizabeth was at this time from home, having
taken their babe William, and gone on a visit to a
relative.

Although, as we have said, the young man was
naturally of a fearless, merry, hopeful nature, his
features were now clouded with care ; and his step,
instead of quickening, became more measured as
he approached home, as though he expected some
unpleasant news or meeting. There was, indeed,
enough in the state of the country and its population to render both old and young thoughtful and
anxious. At the beginning of the reign of George
II. the nation labored under burdens that nearly
destroyed agriculture and repressed all incitement
to industry, and the distress among the laboring
class was terrible. The woollen manufactures were
so depressed that thousands of people had to beg
their bread, and hundreds starved to death. In
respect to the north of Ireland, the most prosperous
part of the country, Primate Boulter thus writes to
the Duke of Newcastle : " We have now had three
bad harvests together, which has made oat-meal, the
great subsistence of the people, dearer than ever."
His Grace then complains of American agents se-
ducing the people with prospects of happier establish-
ments across the Atlantic, and adds, "They have been
better able to seduce people of late by reason of the

necessities of the poor." The Primate then assures the Duke that thirty-one hundred had in the preceding summer gone to the West Indies, and that there were then seven ships lying at Belfast, which were carrying off about a thousand passengers; and "the worst of it is, that it affects only Protestants, and reigns chiefly in the north, the seat of our linen manufactures." The Dissenters also at this time presented a memorial in respect to tithes, as the cause of the emigration. It was the pressure of these calamities that subdued the naturally buoyant temper of the young man, and chastened his step; for he had that day finished his season's work, and knew not, with winter approaching, where to look for more.

As he drew near the threshold, he was espied by one of the little folks who had come to the front of the house in search of turf for the dam, and who, raising the joyful cry, "Hugh has come!" soon brought the whole troop around him. The tallest endeavored to reach his face to kiss him, at the imminent risk of cutting themselves with the sharp axe; others clung to his legs or inserted their hands in his pockets in search of expected and promised presents, while the last comer, seeing little prospect of securing even a finger, set off for the house, screaming at the top of his voice, "Father and mother, Hugh has come!" The shade of sadness on his countenance gave way to a bright smile as the children, some holding by the fingers and others clasping him by the leg, all insisted that he should not stir a step towards the house till he had seen the water-wheel he made for them go. Besides, Aunt Elizabeth was gone away with the baby.

"Who put it in for you?" said Hugh, as, upon receiving this assurance, he put down his axe, and, lifting the youngest to his shoulder, prepared to go with the children, who, delighted, went frisking along and hugging each other in the path before him.

"Father put it in for us," said the eldest boy. "He didn't know as he could do it, because he was busy trying to get his piece out of the loom before Sabbath day; but we got mother to coax him for us, and he found time, and he has got his piece all but out. He will have it out by supper-time. Mother has been helping him. But only see," he exclaimed, pointing to a great stack of weeds, broom, and potato haulm, — "see what a sight of weeds Andrew and I have brought this week; we brought them all on a barrow."

"No, you didn't do it all," cries the little fellow on Hugh's shoulder; "for Jean and I pulled a lot of them."

These weeds, where wood was so scarce, were burnt, and the ashes used to bleach the linen thread.

Leaving Hugh to accompany the children, let us take a survey of the house and adjacent lands. When we say that the abodes of the Protestant

settlers presented a striking contrast to those of the
Irish, both as to comfort and tidiness of appearance,
we would not be understood to imply anything like
the comfort or culture pertaining to the same class
at the present day, but merely relatively; for there
can be no good husbandry where the time of the
farmer is divided between his land and his loom,
as was the custom at that period.   When the mere,
or wild Irish as they were called, were driven out
by James I., and their lands given to Scotch and
English settlers, they retired to inaccessible forests
and bogs with their cattle, where they bred, and
from time to time made attacks upon those who occupied the lands from which they had been driven.
Hence the old soldiers and Scotch from the border
counties and marches, who had been accustomed to
contend with the moss-troopers and the Highland
caterans, and of whom the Irish entertained a salu-
tary dread, were planted on the strong and elevated
lands that commanded the defiles and roads by
which they made their irruptions.   Sir Hugh Mc-
Lellan had received from the crown a grant of
fifteen hundred acres, and erected the building we
have described as both dwelling and fortress; and
here his descendants continued to dwell through
the revolutions of that ruthless period, — at one
time following their superiors to the field as true
liegemen to the king, at others contending for life
and goods with the Irish kernes.   Three times had
the old house been sacked and burnt, but the thick

walls of whinstone, resisting all violence, had been
as often built upon,— till, in 1649, the family, taking up arms with others for Charles, were deprived
of their lands by Cromwell, and driven into Con-
naught.   When the Restoration came, there were
so many new claimants for lands that a compromise
was made, and portions only of forfeited estates
restored, upon which the family again returned to
their possessions, though greatly curtailed, and these,
through the expense of living and the misfortunes of
the times, becoming gradually less and less, Hugh,
the present incumbent, found himself, after the sale
of some lands to discharge old liabilities, possessed
of no more than twelve acres.

And thus, while living in a house conformable to
the state and style of his ancestors, and containing
the relics of other and better days, he was actually
less well to do than many of the occupants of the
mud cottages around him, and only by the severest
toil and the most rigid economy supported his numerous family in thrift and comfort.   Hugh never
set himself above his neighbors on the score that his
ancestors wrote " Sir " before their names, or refused
to labor because his kindred did not ; and he
brought his children up in the same faith, and was
respected and beloved by all the neighborhood.

" Only see," said Hannah Brown to her gossip,
Sandie Wilson, as they were returning from kirk,
" what airs these McLeans do give themselves, just
because they've got a little of this world's gear,

while there is the McLellans, that everybody kens
is a real auld family, never appear to know it; but
that's the way with your real gentry.   And there is
Elizabeth, Hugh's wife, that was brought up a real
lady, out washing her linen at the brook, and scour-
ing flax just like the rest of us, and singing at her
work as though she had not been turned out of
doors and lost a great fortune.''

Hugh, having satisfied the desires of the children,
and escorted by them, now enters the house.   The
great oaken table, at which a company of soldiers
might be seated, stands in the middle of the floor,
where, indeed, it is a fixture.   In a corner of the
huge fireplace sits the mother, a comely woman of
five-and-forty, at her flax-wheel, who greets her
son with an appearance of great affection, which is
as warmly returned.   The father now appears from
another room, — a tall, strongly-built, grave-looking
man, his clothes and beard covered with thrums
from the loom, where he has been weaving.   Alternate work in doors and out had prevented in his
case that pale, sickly look which pertains to the regular weaver.   On the other hand, he was far above
the common size in his proportions, and manifested
in every movement an elasticity and strength evidently undiminished by years.   Indeed, he seemed
a fit representative of those bonnie Scots whose
claymores were so much the dread of the Irish in
the troublous times.   But his great build was still
more strikingly manifested when, the stern features

relaxing into a glad smile of parental affection and welcome, he approached Hugh, and, placing his hand fondly upon his shoulder, in a strong Scotch accent called him his dear bairn, — towering a whole head above him, though Hugh was a large, powerful man.

After the evening meal was finished, the children went to their beds, and the older members of the family were left together. As they sat on the great wooden settle by the turf fire, the mother, who had noticed the disturbed and absent air of her son, inquired if he had heard any bad news during the week, and what made him so downcast.

" Mother," he replied, " there is no news except bad news : there is but one thing talked about by both gentle and simple, and that is the hard times. There is no work to be had now, and they say it will be worse. I heard to-day that in Mitchelster four people had starved to death, and were found dead in the fields with only a little grass in their stomachs. They were reapers, who had been over to England in hopes to get harvest work, but found little, had to beg while there, and starved to death on the way home. I finished my season's work to-day, and know not where to look for more ; and," continued he, laying his hand upon his father's knees, and looking him full in the face, " I have been seriously thinking of going to America ; but I shall take no step without your advice and free consent, nor go without your blessing."

At this abrupt communication the mother's wheel stopped, and she buried her face in her apron. The elder children fixed their eyes eagerly upon their father, who, with an emotion he in vain strove to conceal, sat gazing into the face of his son. An intense painful stillness pervaded the room. Feeling that he was expected to break the silence, he at length said, though with a tremor in his voice that betrayed the severity of the struggle within, " Hugh, you have been an industrious, God-fearing boy, and a dear good son to your mother and me. I know you have not come to this decision without prayer ; and whatever you may decide to do, I make no doubt you will have the blessing of Him who hath said, ' Honor thy father and thy mother, that thy days may be long in the land which the Lord thy God giveth thee.' "

At this implied assent, the mother sobbed aloud. The father's voice trembled, but, recovering himself, he continued with a firmer tone. " You are a young man, and naturally look forward to a settlement in life, — a home and land that you can call your own. These can never be yours in this country. Although, by the blessing of God, we are not in danger of absolute want, yet we are sorely taxed by government, and compelled to support a worship opposed to our consciences. We are harassed by Catholics, Independents, and the Established Church, and between these many mill-stones seem likely to be ground to powder. If you remain, the little you have hardly earned and prudently saved will be eaten up, and then, should times continue hard, you will no longer have the means to go. When I was a child, men began to go to America; many that grew up with me went; none of them have ever returned, although many of them are able to if they wish, for we hear of their prosperity from their relatives here. Some of them own hundreds of acres, who, if they had stayed here, would have lived in a mud hovel, worked out by the day, been buried by the parish, and left no better inheritance to their children after them. It is possible there for a poor man, with nothing but his hands, to own the land he tills; here it is not possible. My thoughts have been a great deal on it as I have sat at my loom, and I doubt not, had I gone there at your age, with all these boys and girls, and worked one half as hard as I have here, it would have been far better for myself and my children. Not that I would complain, having food and raiment while others are starving around me. Therefore, my son, though children are very near, and my heart aches at the thought of separation, yet you may be sure that, in whatever you do, you will have a father's blessing."

He could not bring himself to tell his son he had better go. Hugh crossed over to where his mother, who had been silent during all this conversation, sat beside her wheel, and, putting his arm tenderly around her neck, said, "Mother, don't cry so; I will never go without your free consent."

" You never disobeyed me, Hugh," she replied,
" nor will you now, for I shall not withhold my consent, nor will you go without my blessing.   Surely
I never harbored a thought but for your good ; still,
it is a sore thing for a mother to part with a son
(for we are not so strong in these things as men
are), and to put the wide ocean between her and
the child she has nursed on her bosom.   But what
does Elizabeth say to your purpose ? "

" She does not know it, for it is only within the
week that I have seriously thought of it.   But from
what I heard her say when some of her kindred
went three years agone, and at other times since,
I judge that she will be more for it than myself."

" She has no father or mother, brothers or sisters,
to leave behind ; none nearer of kin than her uncle,
who turned her out of his house and heart for loving you.   She was, I think, but ten years old when
her mother died ; her father was killed by the Irish
kernes in '98, not an arrow-flight from this door.
I was young then, but I mind it well.   It was not
a thing to forget.   He was brought in all bloody,
and laid on this very settle.   He groaned once and
died.   The blood ran from him into the fireplace.
Your grandfather was alive then.   He was an old
soldier and a terrible man with the claymore, and
when the wild Irish got between him and the gate,
he cut his way through them into the court-yard.
All the Protestants fled here for refuge, and I came
with my parents."

" But how is it, Hugh," said the father, " that you
have never mentioned this to us before, and now
seem to have made up your mind at once ? "

" I have long been thinking of it, father, ever
since I knew Elizabeth, and thought of making
her my wife, and of having a home of my own, —
which I well knew, as you have said, I could never
have here. But I thought it would be a hard blow
to mother and you, and I kept my thoughts to my
own breast, and there they have been smouldering
just like these turfs on the fire, and perhaps would
have died out just from pure dislike to mention it to
you ; but the times coming so hard, and my work
failing, brought it all up anew. I finished my job
last night, and this morning received my wages.
Feeling rather sad that I had no other work in prospect, I went to Maggie McDonald's, that keeps the
Stag's Head, to break my fast and take a glass of
beer ; and there I found her house full of good, well-
to-do Scotch people from the county of Cavan, lads
and lasses and auld people, with little children, and
they were bound to Belfast to sail for America. And
they showed me letters they had from their kindred
there, which said that you could buy a farm for the
price of an acre here ; that in many places you could
have land for the settling ; that there were no Irish
or prelatists, but the people were all Protestants,
and they were so far away that the government
permitted them to do much as they pleased ; that,
though the winters were cold, fuel was abundant,

and the soil fruitful ; that there was plenty of game in the woods and fish in the rivers, for there were no dukes or earls to make game-laws ; that if any one didn't have money to buy land, they could have work enough from the other planters till they earned something for themselves ; that although they had to work hard, and suffer some the first few years, they soon became independent, whereas when they were here it was dependence and suffering all the time, with no prospect of change. Now me feeling so down-like, it just stirred up the auld fire, and I have thought of nothing else since. But," he continued, with the caution of a canny Scot, " perhaps I have thought of it ower much, and things are not as they are painted. The tree that blossoms does not always bear ; and I might come to rue the day I stretched out my hand farther than I could draw it back again. But I knew it would not be thus with you, and I determined to be guided by those who had experience, whose heads were cool, and whom it is my bounden duty to obey."

" Well, Hugh," replied the father, " your fathers left bonnie Scotland, and the auld kirk, and kith and kin, and came here to fight with the wild Irish, that they might plant religion here, and have a home and lands of their own, and they got them ; and had it not been for their loyalty to their king, which is no sin to be repented of, their children would have possessed them still. Thus you seem to be ganging the auld gait that they travelled before ye. You

must make up your mind for hardship; and sure I
am that the savages we hear so much about can be no
worse than the wild Irish, by whom so many of your
family were murdered in '41, in the great rebellion.
But it's time we were sleeping, for to-morrow is the
Sabbath of the Lord.   Get the good book, and let
us look to Him without whose blessing nothing
prospers."   He then read the passage that records
Jacob's vow, and remarked, " You will go as poor
as the patriarch, my son, but you go as he did, with
your parents', and I hope with God's, blessing.   I
trust, if He should prosper you in the land you
seek, that, like father Jacob, you will not be un-
mindful of Him who gives us all and is over all."

When Hugh, upon her return, proposed the plan
to Elizabeth, she gave her consent without a moment's hesitation.   " It is but little we have to
fear," she said, "if we only have our health, and
God's blessing, and there is One above we must
look to for that.   Besides your family and a few
others it is little I have to make me regret to leave
this lawless land, where it is always a plague, a
rebellion, or a famine.   There can be no worse than
this, where my father was killed, and my mother
soon followed him from a broken heart.   If we go,
I never expect to see the day I shall not pity those
whom we leave behind.   Besides, when there I am
washing my linen at the brook, or doing any work,
I shall not have my uncle's daughters come strolling
by, tossing their haughty heads, as much as to say,

See what you have come to by marrying below your degree."

This was the only time during her whole life that she ever betrayed that she felt the altered position in which her marriage had placed her; but though she was cheerful as a lark about her work, and probably sang the loudest when her uncle's daughters came by, yet it was too much for poor human nature to endure without inwardly writhing under it. It seems strange to the casual reader, that, in a country so miserably poor as Ireland, marriages should be so frequent and so early. But this grows out of the improvident character of the people, the little reluctance they feel to beggary, and the facility with which the bare means of existence and shelter are procured, and that state of mind which looks and aspires to nothing higher. They go before the priest, and then by the side of some ditch they pile up some mud and stones, and collect furze and sticks to hold up and cover the roof. They then get a pig and go to housekeeping, their only furniture a broken pot. They hire out with the next landlord, if hands are wanted, if not, beg and steal, and thus, with scarce more of expense than a fox or otter, they find a den in which to shelter themselves, and raise up children to pursue the same wretched existence.

But such was not the character of the pair that sat hand in hand, on a pleasant afternoon, by the graves of Elizabeth's parents, talking over the

subject more important to them than all others.
They were of another race, and had received a
different training. They had an ancestry, and an
honorable name to maintain and emulate. They
aspired not merely to existence, a life spent in till-
ing the land of others, but to independence, though
it be unaccompanied by wealth, and is the fruit óf
severe toil; and for this they were willing to risk
much and to suffer much. Hugh had, on the whole,
felt rather disappointed and dissatisfied at the readi-
ness, and, as it had appeared to him at the time,
almost levity with which Elizabeth had assented to
his proposal that she should leave her native country
and go into the wilderness to struggle, far from
friends, with poverty and all the unknown trials of
the emigrant. He well knew her love for him and
her entire confidence in his ability and judgment,
and he feared that, if she had assented upon the
impulse of the moment, and without sufficiently
weighing the difficulties to be encountered and from
which he could not shield her, she might, when the
hour of trial came, give way to corresponding
depression. More especially, as he overheard his
mother say at the time to his father, " Poor girl!
she little knows what is before her, to take a babe
into the wilderness." But his fears were groundless,
and he had yet to learn what material his wife was
made of. For as no hardihood of education can
infuse grit where it is wanting, so neither can luxury
obliterate it when a native element of character.

Elizabeth concealed under a lively temperament and exuberant spirits a keen judgment and great decision of character, with a quick temper and a generous, fearless disposition. Perfectly aware of the determination of her uncle to disinherit her if she married Hugh, she married him, and for his sake deliberately embraced to human view a life of poverty. Her keen perception of character was evinced in the declaration that she had married a man that had the property in himself, which perhaps she meant for a slur upon her uncle's sons, who were all of small capacity, destitute of energy, and lived upon their father. From the time that she made up her mind to marry Hugh, and, as she supposed, poverty, she began to learn to work. She could now spin and weave with the best, could work in doors or out, as was the custom with women of the middle class at that time; she could reap grain, and take care of flax from the pulling to the bleaching. She was superior to the thousand superstitions of the day, and had little fear of warlocks or witches. She would put a piece into the loom, or take up a stocking, or set out on a journey, on Friday, if she wanted to, just as quick as on any other day. Though not in the least inclined to anticipate trouble, but rather to act upon the maxim, Sufficient unto the day is the evil thereof, she was by no means slack in expedients to avert, or resolutions to meet it when at hand.

In reply to all his efforts to make her take a more

4

serious view of their situation, she, divining at once
his apprehensions, exclaimed, giving him a kiss:
"It's no use to talk so to me, Hugh; never fear me;
I am no thoughtless girl. I have seen sorrow and
hardship, and expect to see more. I expect also to
die. I mean to die but once. I don't mean to die
a hundred times through dread of it. That we shall
meet hardships I well know; what they will be, I
don't know and I don't care; but when they come,
we shall have to meet them, and we shall find out
how to do it." Such was the character of the helpmeet Hugh took with him into the wilderness to
struggle for a homestead; and if, as his mother said,
she little knew what was before her, it was very
evident that she feared and cared as little.

Hugh, after this attempt, made no further effort
to impress her with a more serious view of their
situation, except to remark that it was certainly a
sad thing to leave all their relatives and friends, and
go to live among strangers. "So it is indeed,"
replied she; "but they will not be strangers after
we come to live among them. What makes us have
friends here? Because we do right, and love people,
and treat them kindly; and the same kind of
conduct will make friends there that made them
here. Besides, does not the Bible say, that, when a
man's ways please the Lord, he will make even his
enemies to be at peace with him?" It was a
peculiar trait in Elizabeth's character, that, with an
implicit trust in Providence, she always strove by

her own efforts to leave as little for Providence to
do as possible, which often caused her husband to
say that she trusted Providence when she could not
help it.

The time fixed for their departure now drew near.
The two ships were lying at Londonderry, for
passengers. In one of these, the Eagle, Captain
Gilley, they engaged passage. As the ship was to
sail on Monday, many of the relatives and neighbors came in on Sabbath eve to bid the departing
couple good-by. While they were engaged in conversation, Elizabeth, flinging her plaid over her
head, slipped out unnoticed, and in the moonlight
took her way to the churchyard; for, as we have
said, superstitions went for nothing with her.
Here the naturally light-hearted and resolute girl,
kneeling beside the graves of her kindred, sobbed
aloud. Then, as though the dear departed were
present to listen, she exclaimed, " O mother! I shall
never, as I have always hoped to, sleep beside my
father and you. I am going to a far-off land;
there shall I die, and there be buried. But though
I have been a wild and thoughtless girl, I have
tried to serve the God you served, and the Saviour
you taught me to love. God has given me a kind
husband and a sweet babe, and we are going on the
sea; but I believe that covenant-keeping God who,
as you have so often told me, showeth mercy to the
children of his saints till the third and fourth
generation, will be with me there." Then, plucking

a tuft of grass from the grave, she hid it in her
bosom, and rejoined the company without her absence having been observed.

Their relatives accompanied them to the place of
sailing.   One of the vessels was bound to the West
Indies and filled with Irish ; the Eagle, with Scotch.
The Irish, both on board and on shore, made the air
resound with their cries and lamentations.   The
Scotch, on the other hand, said little : a fervent
grasp of the hand, a God bless you, or a silent tear,
was all.   The winter passage was stormy in the
small and crowded ship ; and when a short time out,
she sprang a leak, and they were obliged to put
back.   Setting sail again, they met with heavy
weather, and carried away their rudder-head and
foretop-mast.   Hugh repaired the rudder, and from a
spare spar made a topmast.   As they had lost two
men when the topmast went, and were short-handed,
he assisted in working the ship.   All the worldly
goods that they brought with them, besides their
clothing, of which they had a good stock, were
these : Elizabeth had a feather-bed, and a trammel
and hooks on which to hang a pot, and Hugh had
his tools.   But when the ship sprang a leak they
were flung overboard to lighten, with other cargo.
They then had left only their clothing and provision
for the passage, and ten pounds in gold, which they
determined to keep to buy land, and to part with
only in the last extremity.   The captain was so
much pleased with the conduct of Hugh in repairing

damages and working the ship, that he gave him back his passage money, and in addition made him a present of an axe, adze, and saw, from a lot of new tools which he had brought over as a venture.

Just after making the land, they spoke an outward-bound ship, whose captain told them they would not be allowed to land emigrants from Ireland at Boston, and the captain determined to run for York. The wind, that had been light and baffling all the fore part of the day, now came in strong from the south. All possible sail was made on the ship in order to force her in with the land before night. They soon made a high hill or mountain, which the captain told Hugh was Agamenticus, the ancient name of York, where they were going. As night came on, snow began to fall, mingled with rain, which, freezing as it fell, coated the decks and rigging with ice. The ship, as though instinct with life, and anxious to escape the threatening storm, flew before the wind, and was rapidly nearing the land. Our adventurers vainly strove to pierce the veil of mist which hid from their view the shores of their new home; but they could only perceive a black, undistinguishable mass, upon which the vessel seemed to be madly rushing to destruction. The weather now became rapidly worse; but as the captain was well acquainted with the coast, being a native, and there was a large moon, he determined to run in. Hugh, who had stood his watch with the crew ever since the loss of the two seamen in the gale which carried away the topmast, went below at twelve o'clock, and at three was aroused by the welcome sound of the cable running through the hawse-pipe, as the weary vessel swung quietly at her anchor in York River, where we must leave him for the present, to awake in the morning in the new world which he had chosen for his future home.

CHAPTER III.

WE RISK OUR SCALPS FOR LAND.

IN our last chapter we left Hugh, after the fatigue and excitement of the night, quietly sleeping in York harbor. As day broke, the married pair were on deck and eagerly viewing the shores of the strange land. Strange indeed must all have appeared to them, who had never in all their lives seen anything resembling a grove of trees, — only a few scattered specimens in the parks of the nobility, or the trunks which were dug from the bogs, — and who had scarcely any knowledge of frost or snow, as they gazed upon the vast masses of forest crowning the hills and filling the valleys, the whole country buried in snow, and the ice, through which the vessel under her canvas had pressed, fringing the shores. But as the sun rose, they beheld a spectacle which surpassed all they had ever conceived of beauty, and which, in their new and strange circumstances, produced an impression upon their minds never to be forgotten.

Although it was but moderately cold, the wind being southwest, the frost had congealed the sleet

of the previous night upon the branches and trunks
of the trees on the edge of the forest, and on the
cliffs at the shore, over the whole surface of the
snow, the dwellings of the settlers, and the cordage
of the ship. And when the sun, rising over the
masses of forest that covered the eastern bank
of the river, poured his full radiance upon the landscape, he lighted up the scene with an effulgence
that the eye could scarcely endure, and a beauty
surpassing all description. But to those who beheld
it for the first time, and under such peculiar circumstances, it seemed like enchantment. They looked
at each other as they stood upon the forecastle without the power of speech, and in a sort of maze, as
if to say, " Is this reality, or the work of the fairies
whom we have heard so much about in Ireland ? "

The log-houses of the settlers, every niche and
projection of the rough logs filled with ice, shone
like silver. The frozen gems which overlaid the
branches of the trees were of every imaginable
form ; generally conforming to that of the twigs,
leaves, and buds, but at other times congealed in the
most fanciful shapes, in all that infinitude of variety
which the Creator bestows upon his workmanship.
There were spheres and prisms, diamonds of the
purest water, and masses of network embossed with
silver, from the finest gauze to the coarsest lattice.
In one place were cylinders, in another pyramids.
Here was a long branch flashing in the sunlight, and
extending over the river, from which sprang lesser

ones bristling along their entire length with minute
lances and spangles of pearl.   The hues were as various as the shapes, arising from the different colors
of the materials upon which this fretwork was laid,
and which shone in the clear sunlight through their
crystal covering.   The clear white of the birch,
mottled with specks of gray, and occasionally banded
with stripes of dark red where the elements or the
hand of man had removed the outer bark, contrasted
strikingly with the dark green of the pines, and the
black spruce, and the lighter drapery of the cedars,
the crimson buds of the maple, and the spotted limbs
of the beech.   The bright yellow of the willows,
and the dun of the leaves that still clung to the
branches of the beech and white oak, — the tufts of
many-colored moss on the cliffs, mingled with the
dark purple of the shaggy-barked hemlock, and the
white patches on the trunks of the firs, — all height-
ened in their effect by the dark green of the waters,
which now began to curl beneath the morning
breeze, — completed a picture which no art can imitate, no pen can describe.

A swift trampling is now heard in the forest; a
large moose, roused in his distant lair by the hunters
or the wolves, bursts from beneath the branches of
a hemlock weighed down to the ground by the frozen
sleet, and scattering the icicles far and near, bounds
upon the ice, and, ascending the opposite bank, at a
leap vanishes in the forest; although long after he
has passed from view his course can be traced by the

click of his hoofs, the falling icicles, and the whir of the partridge roused by his passage.

So quickly did he burst upon them and disappear, that they had only time to notice his huge, mis-shapen head, his immense height, the tuft beneath his throat, and his great horns.

" What in the name of heaven is that, — a bear? " cried Hugh to the mate ; who replied, smiling, that it was a moose.

" Will it bite? " said Hugh.

" No ; but it will kill a man with its fore-feet if it hits him," replied the mate, who then explained to Hugh the nature and habits of the creature.

" Well," continued Hugh, glancing again at the forest, from which, moved by the wind and thawed by the sun, the ice was beginning to fall in showers, " whatever hardships I may suffer in this country, (and I don't expect they will be few,) I never shall forget how handsome this looked."

" Hardship won't hurt you," replied the mate ; " you are one of the *hard-meated* kind ; your arm feels like the branch of an oak-tree. I only wish I had your strength. Wouldn't I keep sailors in order ! "

While they were speaking, four Indians, with rifles and snow-shoes on their backs, suddenly came from beneath the hemlock, and followed on at a loping trot in the track of the moose.

" They will never catch that moose, — never in the world," said Hugh. " Why, they don't go one half as fast as he does."

"Yes, they will," said the mate. "In a short time the crust will thaw and let him through, and cut his legs so that he can't run, and then they will put on their snow-shoes and catch him."

Elizabeth and Hugh had heard so much of Indians and their cruelties, and seen so many pictures of them, that they recognized them at once, and gazed with great interest upon those receding beings, of whose character and habits they were to have so sad an experience.

As the captain had refunded Hugh his passage-money, he had now a little to help himself with till he could look about and till spring. By the captain's direction he went to the house of a settler named Riggs, who agreed to let him have a room for the winter. He borrowed a hand-sled and hauled up his goods and tools, and Riggs invited them to dine. Mrs. Riggs at once "took to" Elizabeth, and the children were delighted with the baby.

After dinner they sat down before a fireplace as large as that in the old house in Ireland, which was built hundreds of years ago, when there was wood in that country, and when the great families on occasion roasted oxen whole; but instead of a little smouldering fire of turf, this was filled with great logs of wood, which sent the blaze roaring up the great chimney. Riggs, who was a well-to-do farmer, with a family of rugged boys, brought up from the cellar a great pitcher of cider and some apples, and offered Hugh and Elizabeth a pipe, and they sat down to talk and get acquainted.

As the host had been born in the country, and had cleared up his farm from the forest, he was fully competent to tell Hugh and his wife all they wanted to know, and all the methods of getting along in a new country.

"It will be much better for you," said he, "to work out awhile before attempting to farm for yourself. You will thus save yourself from a great many mistakes, and much needless labor by reason of taking hold of things by the wrong end, and will gain experience that will be worth to you more than money."

Hugh saw the reasonableness of this advice, and determined to act upon it. He then, as fire was the first requisite, asked where he could buy some wood.

"Wood?" replied the other; "help yourself anywhere. We are glad to burn it up here to get rid of it. And now, as you are a carpenter, and the boys and I are not over handy with tools, if you will make me a pair of bob-sleds, we will haul you wood enough to last all winter."

"I will gladly make them," said Hugh, "if you will give me the pattern."

They then ground the tools, while the boys set off for the woods, and before night he had a load of wood at the door, a fire burning, and a few utensils for cooking procured. Elizabeth had washed the room, and made up a bed on the floor in one corner. Mrs. Riggs lent them a table and a wooden settle; and that night they sat down by a cheerful fire to supper in their own room, safe from the perils of the sea, and with grateful hearts to Him who had preserved them.

Hugh soon had proof of the report that there was work for all in America. The captain employed him to unhang the ship's rudder and repair it in a more thorough manner than he had been able to do at sea, and also to make a new top-mast and top-gallant-mast, and a new pawlbit to the windlass, and to do some calking on the ship's upper works. As carpenters in Europe often in those days learned the calker's trade, he was thus enabled to do the whole. In the meantime his wife procured a wheel, and began to spin flax and wool, and exchange the yarn for provisions; and every night when Hugh came home from his work, his ears were saluted with the familiar sound of the wheel. The first stormy day he made a bedstead, which raised them off the floor; and after that, at different times, a table, a high-backed settle, and some chairs bottomed with basket-work.

When the ship was done, he hired himself with a gang of men to go into the woods to cut spars. He had never seen a tree cut in his life, but doing as he saw the rest do, he became in the course of the winter so expert in the use of the narrow axe, to which he had never before been accustomed, that not a man in the gang could take the heart of a tree from him.

When the snow went off in the spring, he let himself to his neighbors; at one time he was employed in clearing land, at another in burning, cutting, and piling the logs for the second "burn," hacking in the crop, and fencing. Thus he became familiar with and an adept in all parts of the pioneer's life. Elizabeth, in the meanwhile, spun and wove for the neighbors, and learned from them the art of making leggings and breeches of deer and moose hide.

He had not been long in his new abode before the selectmen came to see him to find out what he was, for they had a custom, in those days, of warning all persons of idle and poor character out of town, lest they should become an expense to the townsfolk or cast discredit upon them. He frankly told them that he was a Presbyterian; that he left Ireland to escape persecution, and to obtain a home for himself and family; that he had attended their meetings, and been fed with the bread of life, and should cordially unite with them in the worship of God. This declaration melted the crust of the Puritan heart like frost in the sunshine, and he at once found himself admitted to the confidence of the community.

Thus, by prudence and industry, our immigrants husbanded their little stock of money, learned the habits of the country, the modes of doing business, and the most profitable methods of labor. They made many valuable friends, and established a good character among their neighbors.

In the fall Hugh was invited by his brother James, who had been some years in the country, to come to Saco and cut masts. Leaving his family at York, he spent the winter in the woods. In the spring he moved his family into the house with his brother, and worked for him through the summer. The next year he moved to Back Cove in Falmouth, and by permission built a log-house, and cleared a piece of land, and then by what he could raise and obtain by his work lived comfortably. Scarcely was he settled here before he was driven off by the Indians, and obliged to flee for safety to Portland; his house was burnt, but he saved a horse and cow, though all their clothing and household stuff were lost. What little money he had earned was expended in replacing his tools and their housekeeping necessaries; so that the family were now thrown back upon the ten pounds which, through all their trials, they had kept as a sacred trust to buy land. But with indomitable resolution he went to work in Portland, still hoping for a home, which now seemed further off than ever. The dread of the savages, who had wasted the whole eastern shore of Maine with fire and slaughter, had heretofore caused the settlements to be made upon the shore, both as being less exposed to attack, and as affording fish for food and enabling the settlers to obtain hay and pasture from the salt marshes while clearing their land.

But Portland was now rapidly recovering from the effects of the Indian wars. Masts, and fish, and lumber were exported in large quantities, ships were built, and a back line of lots was in the process of laying out. Work was plenty, and Hugh was able to support his family comfortably; but money was scarce and hard to be obtained, nearly all trade being by barter. But land in any safe and desirable position could not be obtained without money, and their great desire — amounting almost to anguish — was for land. No American born and bred can realize the uncontrollable desire cherished by the poorer classes of Europe, who have been tenants for generations, to become themselves owners of land, — to have a spot they can call their own! It was especially strong in the breasts of Hugh and Elizabeth. But to continue in this way, accumulating but a trifle above their living, seemed to afford but a wretched prospect of ever obtaining enough to purchase land, cheap as it was held in the colonies. For several weeks this Christian mother, Elizabeth, as she lay on her bed, kept from sleep by anxious thoughts, revolved their situation in her mind; and often during that period, as she afterwards said, she rose in the night and prayed for direction and support. At length she came to a decision which she lost no time in making known to her husband.

"Hugh," said she, the next night, after supper was over and the children abed, "what man was that you were talking to so long the other day at the wood-pile?"

" What day ? "

" Why, the day you stayed at home to cut wood."

" O, that was more than a fortnight ago."

" No matter; who was he ? "

" I don't know his name."

" How provoking you are! What was his business with you ? "

" Well, that was a man who is going to settle in Narragansett No. 7." *

" Where is that ? "

" Nine or ten miles back in the woods. The government has given a township to the men who fought in the Narragansett war, and their heirs. This man has his father's share, and he is going to settle on it ; and he has bought out some others."

" I suppose the government has given this land to these men, just as King James gave land to our people who fought against the French and Papists, because he hadn't money to pay them, Hugh ? "

" Just so. He tells me that a good many of these people have farms in Massachusetts, and don't need to go into the woods and endure hardship, and run the risk of being killed by the Indians, and so they sell their rights very cheap. He has bought some rights for a mere song. He says the land is excellent, and heavily timbered."

" What risk is there from Indians ? Are we not at peace with them, and haven't they signed the treaty ? "

* What is now Gorham, the scene of our story.

5

"Yes; but many think they can't be trusted, and say they are sullen, and, when in liquor, threaten. My brother James says they are plotting something, and will break out before long. This is the general feeling, I find; and that is the reason for these Narragansett lands being sold so cheap, because people don't like to leave the sea-shore and the places where there are garrisons, and where they are safe from the Indians."

"I thought you talked with him a good while."

"Yes, I talked with him some time."

"That was more than a fortnight — yes, it was nearly three weeks — ago, and you never said one word to me about it, Hugh!"

"Well, I don't know as I did."

"Hugh," said she, rising and placing her hand on his shoulder, "do you want me to tell your thoughts? You talked a good hour with that man, and more, — for I was spinning where I could see you, and I knew by the thread I spun; and you were in real earnest. You found that the land was cheap, and came within your means, and yet you never mentioned it to me. I know that you saw this was a better chance than you have ever had, or ever will have again; but you kept it to yourself, because you wouldn't expose me and the children to the Indians, and thought I would be for going."

"Betsy," replied he, putting his arms around her, and taking her upon his knee, "you are a witch! That *is* just the reason why I said nothing about it;

and I have tried to put all thought of it out of my mind; but I can't, — it haunts me night and day."

" That is what you have been thinking about with your head between your hands, while I have been washing the dishes."

" Yes, Betsy."

" I had an inkling of this. William overheard your talk, and told me part, and I guessed the rest from your looks. Now, Hugh, I say, go! All the time you have been poring over this, I also, unknown to you, have been thinking about it and praying to God. It seems to me that we are placed just like this: if we had had money enough, we could have bought land at home." Her eyes filled with tears at the familiar word, but she brushed them away, and continued: " If we had money, we could also buy land here in Falmouth, and have schools for our children, and the preaching of the Word, and have neighbors, and be safe, because this safety and these good things cost money. But here is a piece of land that is offered for a very little money, — just what we have got, — and the balance in blood, and risk, and hardship. Now, money is just what we have the least of; but we are rich in the other things. We have health, and strength, and resolution; and I say, let us go up and take the land and possess it, and make a home for ourselves and our children. We have suffered a great deal; let us stick to it and gain our object, and not lose the good of all we have gone through."

" You are a brave, good lass," said Hugh, pressing
her to his bosom ; " but have you considered the
difference between living here and in the woods,
with a few families, miles apart, so that the Indians
can cut them off one by one ? "

" Well, Hugh, I say, 'Sufficient unto the day is
the evil thereof.' The people who are going are
Massachusetts people, born in the country, used to
hardship, used to Indians and to fighting them. I
am sure the people that have killed Philip and destroyed the Narragansetts can take care of these
Indians, who have had some severe lessons already.
I say, if land can be bought for danger and for hardship, that is the chance for us, who have not much
else to pay down."

" But have we a right to expose the lives of the
little ones? "

" That is where the greatest trouble has been with
me," said his wife; " but I have turned it over in
my mind, and carried the matter to my Maker, and
I feel clear that we should go, and leave the rest
with Him."

" That is just the way I have felt from the first,"
said Hugh, drawing a long breath, as though relieved
of a heavy burden ; " but I did not like to expose
you and the children to risks that I would cheerfully
take myself. Had I come over here as my brother
James did, a young man and single, I would have
ground my axe and started by sunrise the very next
morning after I heard of such a chance at night. But

as we have both been brought to think alike without
saying anything to each other, I take it to be God's
will that this should be our path; and by his blessing we will walk therein."

This Narragansett No. 7 was a lot of wilderness
land given by the State of Massachusetts to Captain
Shubael Gorham and one hundred and nineteen others, for their services in King Philip's war, and was
called for him Gorhamtown. But it was a town
only in name. It had been surveyed for settlement;
and here and there a logging road ran through the
woods, made by lumbermen, who in the winter
months, when there was no danger from the savages,
came to cut timber, and haul it to the Presumpscot
River. It is not certain whether there were only
two families in the place, — Captain John Phinney's
and John Ayres's, — or whether there was another,
James Mosier's. Thus, with the exception of these
families, it was an unbroken forest, a thoroughfare
of the Indians as they came to the sea-coast to hunt,
fish, and trade skins in time of peace, and in time of
war to harass and kill the settlers. It was nine miles
from Portland, and reached only by a path through
the woods.

The morning after this conversation, Hugh started
for Narragansett, and spent nearly a week exploring
the different lots which he knew were for sale, in
company with a young man who had carried the
chain for the surveyor, and who knew the corners
of the lots. Just as night drew on, they came upon

the hill where the academy now stands; and seeing
a smoke rising up among the trees below them, they
followed its direction, and came to the camp of John
Ayres, which stood where the brick house which we
have mentioned now stands. He cultivated no land,
abhorred the axe and every kind of regular work,
but lived by trapping, hunting, and fishing. He was
at home, made them welcome, and, having just killed
a deer, was able to entertain them bountifully.

Hugh McLellan was a man who, besides possess-
ing a deep religious faith and fearless nature, always took hold of things by the right end; everything that he touched prospered. This arose from
an excellent judgment, great strength of body, and
a patient, hopeful nature. He soon found that the
spot where he was now was the one most suitable
for him; and after spending the next day in exploring it, told Ayres, on his return to the camp at night,
that he should buy it, and move in during the latter
part of winter or in the early spring.

"Well, then," said Ayres, "as I am only a squat-
ter, I suppose I must make tracks."

"By no means," replied Hugh; "neighbors are
not so plenty. I should be very sorry to have you
go away, and shall be very glad to have you stay as
long as you wish. There is room for both of us, and
many more."

He found the place well watered by springs, and
the brook, which is now a mere thread, was then
large, and afforded trout in plenty. The high land

was covered with an enormous growth of maple, yellow birch, and oak. The ravines and banks of the brook were filled with hemlock, pine, and ash. But that which principally attracted his attention and decided his choice was the great size and straight growth of the white pines, which, mixed with a few hemlocks, covered the swales and slopes of the hills, and were scattered here and there among the hardwood trees, and which were suitable for the masts of the largest ships of war. Masts for large ships are now made of several pieces, clustered round a central core, and hooped together, because the country does not now afford trees of sufficient size to make them in one piece; but then they were made of a single tree.

In those days, when the States were colonies of Great Britain, the Royal Commissioner of Forests employed surveyors who went through the woods and marked with a broad arrow every sound and straight pine over thirty-six inches in diameter. These were reserved for the king's ships, and the owner of the land whereon they grew could not cut or sell them. But the government would pay him liberally to cut and haul them to the landing. They were tremendous trees, some of them more than four feet through; and to fell and haul them through the woods with the wooden-shod sleds and small cattle of that period, fed entirely on hay, and often merely by browsing, was an enterprise that might well daunt the boldest. But Hugh was no

common man ; he saw that the masts were of the
best quality, and would command their price in cash
could they be transported to the coast ; and he felt
himself equal to the task. He also saw, further than
this, that all around were rivers and brooks which afforded mill-sites, — Presumpscot on the east, Stroudwater on the south, and still another on the west.
There were also smaller affluents, which at that day,
when all the springs shaded by forests were full,
afforded at a trifling outlay moderate water-powers.
Thus, while the masts and other spars could be made
directly available, the remaining timber would become more valuable each year, as population increased, roads were made, and mills were built.
Here he determined to make his clearing, and to
labor for a home for himself and family.   There
were, as has been said, but two permanent settlers
besides himself — Phinney and Mosier — on the
whole tract (for Ayres was a mere hunter and tran-
sient dweller), — one of them about a mile distant,
the other more than two miles.   Except their clear-
ings, all was an unbroken forest to the sea and back
to Canada ; while it was directly in the Indian trail
that led from Canada to the sea-coast, whither the
Indians in great numbers resorted in the spring,
summer, and autumn, for fishing and hunting, and
to spear salmon, and in many places to raise corn.

Hugh now returned to his family, secured the
land, and, as it was late in the fall, found work upon
a vessel during the winter. In the last week in

February he left his work, and, with his pack and axe, started on snow-shoes for the woods. Upon the easterly side of the road leading to Fort Hill, and opposite to where the brick house now stands, upon land now occupied by Asa Palmer, Esq., he found an old logging camp, with the roof fallen in and filled with snow and leaves of trees. The great logs of which the walls were built had resisted the force of the elements and the hand of Time. Several hands, it was evident, had been required to roll up these logs, and the camp was of a size sufficient to contain a number of men. Hugh beheld these evidences of former occupation with that interest which men always feel who are about to undertake a perilous enterprise, as they trace the footsteps of those who have preceded them in like efforts. So long had it been abandoned, that a clump of young trees had grown up within the walls of the camp, and almost obliterated all evidences of the pioneers' operations. But with a practised eye he traced through the young growth the road by which the masts had been hauled, and that to the spring where the lumbermen had obtained their water. He searched out the decaying stumps of the trees they had cut, and by the withered stalks of clover and other grass, and of weeds foreign to the woods, ascertained the place where stood the hovel for their cattle. Having now satisfied his curiosity, he returned to the camp, and proceeded to cut the young trees and bushes that grew within it; then, using his snow-shoes for shovels, he began to clear it of snow. While thus engaged, his thoughts involuntarily reverted to those who had built and occupied the structure before him.

" It is many a long year since these pines were cut and men slept in this old ruin," said Hugh to himself.

While busied with these thoughts, and scraping the snow along the sides of the camp, he came upon an Indian tomahawk buried in the sides of one of the logs that formed the end wall; the handle had decayed and fallen away, and the stem of a blackberry-bush had sprung from the moss and dead bark of the log, and grown through the empty eye. As he stood thus, alone in the wilderness, and held this emblem of savage hostility and ruthless barbarity in his hand, even his firm mind was not proof against uneasy thoughts. Involuntarily the idea would intrude that the gang of the camp had been killed by the Indians, and he almost expected to find their bones among the leaves. It was impossible to prevent the thought, " Such may be my fate and that of my family."

Having completed his task, he got together some dead wood and brush, and made a great fire in the middle of the camp, thus burning up all the impurities and the green moss on the walls, and making the whole place dry and wholesome. As he had no tools to make splints and shingles, and bark would not run at that time of the year, he was compelled to

THE DESERTED CAMP.   Page 74.

cover the roof with brush.   As the ends were standing, he made rafters of poles, and covered them with
the brush, laying it in courses like shingles, placing
the tops of the branches uppermost and lapping over.
He then put other poles upon the brush, to prevent
the wind from blowing it away, fastening them down
with wooden pins, and leaving a large hole in the
middle for the smoke to make its escape through.
Thus he made quite a tight roof.   Next, he hewed
out some planks from a pine sapling, pinned them
together for a door, and hung it on wooden hinges.
He then covered the ground with hemlock boughs,
upon which he spread his blanket for a bed.

"A man might as well take all the comfort he
can," said Hugh; so, driving four stakes into the
floor before the fire, he piled up some logs between
them, and spread his blanket over them to lean his
back against.

Having eaten his supper, he sat down, and, leaning his back against the logs, took his axe between
his knees and began to whet it with a stone (for he
had no grindstone), that he might be ready for the
morrow's labor.

" It is good enough for a king," said he, stretching
out his hands and feet to the blaze, and looking
around upon the walls, now dry and lighted up by
the fire.   "This is what I call real comfort.   If the
children and their mother were only here, it would
be perfect."

His first work was to fell trees for a "burn"; and

as the sap had begun to flow, he made a trough, and, sticking his axe into a rock-maple, put a chip in the gash to guide the juice, and so had maple-sap to drink while at work.

It was now the latter part of March, and he determined to go for his family, who were all ready and waiting to join him. They set out from Portland at daybreak, cheerful and with light hearts, although they would have been objects of pity to any person they might have chanced to meet. Elizabeth rode on the white horse, carrying one child; William drove the cow; and Hugh followed, with a pack on his back and a little girl in his arms. Elizabeth had on the horse with herself nearly all their household stock.

They arrived at the camp late in the afternoon, as they travelled but slowly, cumbered with children and cattle. But when they arrived they found a heavy snow had fallen and broken in the roof, and filled the camp with snow. It was a sad disappointment; the children were crying with cold and hunger; they themselves were fatigued; and it was all the more bitter because Hugh had on the road told them how comfortable his abode was, and how he had a great fire ready to kindle the moment they arrived, and the little ones, with the eagerness of children for change, had been pleasing themselves with anticipations of the good times and great fires they were to have in the new camp.

But nothing daunted, Hugh kindled a fire beneath

the root of a windfallen tree that sheltered them from the wind; Elizabeth milked the cow and gave them all a drink; and leaving William to mind the smaller ones by the fire, the pair set resolutely at work, removed the snow, put some brush on the roof, made a fire, and, spreading down some quilts to keep the children from freezing their feet (for they were all barefoot), and huddling all together for warmth, lay down by the fire to rest.

"This is a sorry time for you and the children, Betsy," said Hugh.

"Indeed, we've much to be thankful for," she replied, with her cheerful temper that it was not in the power of circumstances to repress; "we've wood enough, and no rent to pay, thank God; and the children don't mind it. I've known a poor creature's pig seized and his pot taken off the fire in Ireland (thank God we're not there!) for the rent of a place not half so good as this, and not two rods of land with it! Sure, it's our own; and home is home, they say, be it ever so homely."

The sun rose bright the next morning, with a warm southwest wind. Hugh got up early, made a good fire, and brought in some sap and spruce-gum for the children; the snow melted away from the door and ran into the brook, and they could play out of doors. They were therefore in high glee, and all were cheerful and happy.

"It don't take much to make children happy," said Hugh to his wife, as he glanced at their smiling faces and healthy, robust forms.

"Not if they have but little," she replied. "But
there are the children of rich people, who have
everything that can be imagined, and one would
think ought to be happy; they are never satisfied,
always fretful, while ours are contented with spruce-
gum and maple-sap."

"I think, then, poor people's children are best
off," said Hugh.

"To be sure they are," replied Elizabeth; "that
is, if they have food and clothing, and could only be
brought to believe it. And you know yourself that
the children who are brought up in a hard, rough
way, always make the brightest and smartest men.
Look at our William, he has seen hard times ever
since he was born, and where can you find a boy
of his age like him among the children of the rich?
How much more he is worth for getting along in the
world than my uncle's boys in Ireland, who have
always had all they wanted, and who, because they
have had it, are feckless and do-nothings. I might
have been the same," she continued, "if I hadn't
been lucky enough to marry a poor man;" and
the lively creature laughed and clapped her hands
with a heartfelt merriment that was contagious, and
in which Hugh and all the children joined her.
Then, rising up, she said, "While I feel so happy,
I'm going over to see the woman in the other camp,
and get acquainted with my neighbors."

Having now his tools, Hugh split out shingles
four feet long, and, putting them on rough, made

the roof tight; while William, who was now eight years old, filled the chinks between the logs with clay from the brook, and, piling up brush around the bottom logs, made the place really warm and comfortable. Till this time they had been obliged to keep the horse and cow in the camp at night, for fear of the wolves and bears, to the great delight of the children, who, every time their mother's back was turned, would get a little milk, which made her wonder why the cow gave so little, for the rogues kept their own counsel, and so the falling off was imputed to driving her from Portland.

But their father now made a hovel of large logs that the wolves could not get into. He then brought from Portland the wool and flax wheels. To be sure, they raised no flax or wool. But Hugh oftentimes, when he could not obtain money for his work, took wool or flax for pay, and his wife spun and knit up the wool into stockings and mittens for him and the children, and spun the flax, and then carried it to Portland to his cousin Bryce McLellan, who was a weaver by trade, and who wove it in his loom. Such shifts were they put to at that time to get along. Sometimes, also, she took flax and wool home to spin for other folks, and had a proportion of it for spinning it.

They now had a piece of land, and it was paid for, and was their own. But to pay for it had taken the last penny. They had not a chair, stool, nor table; for when the Indians burnt their camp at

Back Cove, they lost everything ; and when they
lived in Portland, in the house with Jennie Miller,
who was a relation, they used her things.   Hugh had
as yet no time to make them, because he must spend
all the time possible in cutting down trees, by which
they might get their bread.   They had but a fortnight's provisions for themselves ; not a lock of hay
for the cow or the horse, although it was yet only
the middle of March ; no bedstead, for they slept on
brush laid on the ground.   They needed neither
churn nor milk-pans, for they drank the milk as fast
as it came from the cow.   They sat on the floor, and
ate off of the floor ; but Hugh said that was what
half of Ireland did.   They had not a bit of earthen,
tin, or crockery in the camp, but ate from plates of
wood made with an axe and adze, and with wooden
spoons.   They had neither tea nor coffee pot, because they had no tea or coffee ; no candles or lamps,
for they had but one room, and the fire made it light
as day ; and when they wanted a light in the night,
they took a pine knot or a piece of pitchy wood.
They had not a fowl of any kind, for they had no
grain to feed it on.   But they were a living exem-
plification of the truth of the proverb, " Where
there 's a will there 's a way."   The horse and cow
picked up a living by means of the great quantities
of " browse " afforded by the trees that were felled
for clearing, and the old grass that was on the banks
of the brook and in the open places of the woods ;
while the fear of wolves always brought them home

at night. Notwithstanding, they were cheerful,
resolute, and happy, because they trusted in God,
and believed that he would crown their endeavors
with success. Poor as they were, they had the Bible,
the Catechism, and a few other good books. Night
and morning from that humble camp went up the
voice of praise and heartfelt thanksgiving to God;
and the Ministering Angel passed by many a lordly
palace and luxurious abode to hover in benediction
over the rude camp of the immigrant in the wilderness. They were strong of limb, strong in faith,
strong in God, — these descendants of those who
read their Bibles among the hills of Scotland, with
the broadsword holding down the leaves against the
breeze, and who fought against Claverhouse. By
degrees they obtained the things of prime necessity.
Hugh went to Stroudwater, bought some boards, cut
them up, laid them across the horse's back, and thus
brought them home, and made a table. He hewed
out a plank settle, and made a back to it of small
poles; split out some stools from a large log, and
put legs to them. Every stormy day that he could
not work, he made some article of necessity for the
camp. Meanwhile the children collected sap, and
Elizabeth made sugar, which they used or sold to
the Indians (who, though they made it themselves,
could never have enough of it) for meat and fish.
Hugh continued to fell trees, and when he got out
of provisions and could do no better, went out to
work at Saco or Portland, to get a little corn, and

6

brought it home on his back; and when by good
fortune it was more than he could thus bring, William or his mother went with the horse.

It was now late in April, and as the trees cut then
would be too green to burn, Hugh went out to work
till June, when it was time to burn the fallen timber, in order that he might obtain provisions to last
him through his planting, when he must be at home.
Here we shall leave him for the present, with wishes
for his success.

CHAPTER IV.

THE FIRST CROP.

THE long-expected month of June came at last, and the weather was most propitious, for the month of May had been a very dry month, and the dry weather continued, which was of great consequence to Hugh, as his timber had been cut late and was green, while the success of his crop depended upon a good "burn" to consume the roots and leaves, and have a good bed of ashes to plant on.

It was a time of great interest with the children, — the burn, — and indeed with all of them, as their bread depended upon it. By daybreak they were astir; indeed, Billy had been up and out of doors two or three times in the night to see if it was daylight. They hastily dispatched their breakfast, and then moved everything in the camp over the brook, lest, it being a dry time, the fire should run into the woods. Most terrible conflagrations have been, and are still, in the eastern parts of Maine, caused in this way. When all was prepared, Hugh and Elizabeth and William, each with a firebrand, approached the edge of the clearing that was driest, — being that which was cut in the winter, — and waving the brands over their heads till they blazed, flung them among the dry leaves. In an instant forked tongues of flames sprang up, and the fire, fanned by a light breeze that came up with the sun, roared and ran with the speed of a race-horse before the wind. The children clapped their hands and danced about for joy. The parents looked gravely on, for there was danger of its running. But happily the greater part of the fuel was in a few hours reduced to ashes without damage, and Hugh, walking over it the next morning, after it had cooled, joyfully pronounced it a good burn.

But the children were not so well satisfied with the result as their parents. It had been a great and glorious jubilee amid the monotony of their lonely life, and they could not feel at all satisfied that it should last no longer. The forest in its original state had been thickly peopled with wild animals of various kinds, of which the greater portion yet remained. When the fire was well kindled, Hugh told the children to go to the farther end of the clearing and they would see some fun; and to keep them out of the track of the fire, their mother went with them. No sooner had the flames and smoke begun to drive through the timber, than its inhabitants took the alarm, and such a scampering as there was! It was a curious sight to behold. There were raccoons, woodchucks, rabbits, skunks, porcupines, partridges, foxes, and field-mice in armies "on the clean jump," all running for dear life to gain the shelter of the forest, while a great gray wolf, which had been taking a nap beneath the fallen trees, brought up the rear.

Hugh, who, in expectation of some such guest, had brought his gun with him, fired, and the ball cut through his backbone; still the hard-lived savage, bracing himself upon his fore-feet, while his hind parts were useless, snarled, and showed his teeth till Hugh dispatched him with blows from the breech of the gun. "Take that, and that, and that, my gentleman," said Hugh. "You are the fellow that chased the horse the other night."

The flight of the smaller animals, and the death of the wolf, had put the children almost beside themselves with mingled terror and wonder, and when the spectacle passed away so rapidly, it produced a corresponding depression. They walked round the wolf, first at a respectful distance, for they were afraid he might come to life; and Billy moving his tail with a stick, it made Abigail run and scream as though he was after her. But gradually they grew bolder, till Billy finally kicked him, and Abigail threw dust in his face.

"Why, mother," said Billy, sitting down disconsolate at the door of the camp, "I thought it would have lasted two or three days."

"And I too," said Abigail; "I thought it would be so handsome to see it burn in the dark nights."

It was now somewhat difficult to decide what to
do with the land. The proper way would have
been for Hugh to go upon the land in the latter
part of May, and begin to cut down trees, and so to
continue through the month of June. Then tho
trees and the stumps would have "bled" (or given
out their juices) freely, and have become, in the
long, hot summer, exceeding dry; and also, as the
trees would then have been in full leaf, the leaves
would have remained on, and, being dry, would
have made the fire burn very much better. The
stumps of the trees, too, would have bled so freely
that they would not have sprouted so much the next
year. Then, by setting his fire in the autumn,
Hugh could have burnt cleaner, and the land would
have been in excellent order for sowing with winter
rye, or (early in the spring) with grain or with
corn; whereas — though by the dryness of the
spring he had got a good burn — it was now the
10th of June, and late to plant corn, as, the country
being covered with forest, the frosts came early in
those days.

But the fact was, they were almost starving for
bread, and, having now a piece of land of his own,
Hugh had become tired of going great distances to
work for food, and of bringing it home on his back;
so he determined, although it was late, to force a
crop, and, with his usual good judgment, he succeeded. He made the holes with a stake, the children dropped into them the corn and pumpkin-

seeds, and he covered them with his foot. Part of
the ground he sowed with peas, and on some spots,
where it was very mellow and without many roots,
he planted potatoes, because he said that it was not
good to have all your eggs in one basket, and that,
if one crop failed, the other might do something.
The ground was naturally warm, and, being covered
with a thick coat of hot ashes, forced the crop
along, and they were soon assured of a bountiful
harvest. Hugh, the moment his seed was in, went
into the woods to fell trees for the next year's burn,
that he might have it ready at the proper time.
The cow — now having in addition to the grass an
abundance of "browse" from the trees which Hugh
was cutting, and which were now in full leaf — began to increase her gift of milk, so that the children
had abundance, and the parents often came in for a
share.

The little money Hugh had from time to time
received for his labor was husbanded to the utmost
extent for use in case of sickness or accident, and
also to enable them to obtain what seemed to be
the foundation of all progress with them, a yoke of
oxen. The wife and Billy would go to the brook,
or through the woods to the Presumpscot River, and
catch fish. They got sometimes meat from the Indians in exchange for milk ; raccoons and partridges
were also plentiful in the woods; and Hugh, who
always took his gun with him into the woods, would
often shoot a partridge or porcupine, or come across
a coon in a hollow tree.

Every effort was made by Billy and his mother
either to procure food or to do without it, in order
not to oblige the father to leave his labor in the
woods, as every tree cut was so much towards a
harvest the next year. Elizabeth even learned to
use an axe, and, as she was possessed of the strength
of a man, assisted her husband to no small extent
in chopping. Billy also had a light axe, and now
began to chop a little. As Hugh had no grindstone, but had to go nearly a mile to Captain
Phinney's to grind his axe, Elizabeth would take
William and go there, and grind one axe while he
was chopping with the other.

As it was now almost impossible to work in the
woods by reason of the black flies, midges, and
mosquitoes, (Hugh coming home some nights as
bloody as a butcher from their stings,) he went to
Portland to work. It was determined between
them before he set out, that, if they got out of provisions, William or Abigail, who could now ride a
horse, was to let him know, in order that none of
the money he earned might be expended without
absolute necessity; otherwise he was to remain at
his labor.

Though so poor themselves, they often found
opportunity to exercise hospitality. The brooks
and streams in the neighborhood were the resort of
beavers and muskrats; hedgehogs, of which the
Indians also make great use, were abundant in the
hard-wood growth, as they feed on the bark of

trees; and salmon and other fish were numerous. This attracted the Indians, who had a sort of summer residence at Gambo, a few miles off, where they had a cornfield, and they were often camping by the brook below the house. Elizabeth often treated them to a drink of milk, though in so doing she sometimes pinched herself; or gave them food or a piece of tobacco; or spun for the squaws a little thread, which they valued very highly, it being much better than deer-sinew for stringing their beads and working their moccasins; and when overtaken by storms, they often spread their blankets at her fire. The Indians, with whom it is always a fast or a feast, were not by any means backward, when they had been successful in hunting or fishing, about returning these favors. She also obtained from them a great deal of valuable information about the preservation of food, and shifts whereby to get along in emergencies. As for William and Abigail, they went back and forth to the Indian wigwams, and played in the brook with their children, and slid down hill with them, in the winter, on pieces of birch-bark, and ate with them, if they happened to be eating, — for the savages are not regular about their meals, but eat when they are hungry or when they can get food, — and would no more hesitate to ask food from one old Indian squaw, who was often at the camp after thread, than from their mother, and thus were on the best of terms with all the Indians round.

One morning, in the latter part of July, Ayres's
wife came into the camp in great agitation. Though
a very kind, prudent, and industrious woman, she was
timid, and had a nervous apprehension of Indians.
" Have you heard the news? " said she, dropping
into her seat and clasping her hands over her bosom,
and then asking for a drink of water.

Elizabeth gave her the water, and then inquired,
" What news ? "

" Why, about the Indians! "

Going to the door, Elizabeth told the children
they might go down and play with the Indians; and
when they were out of hearing she said to her visitor, " Now tell your news. I was afraid the children would hear and tell it all over again to the
Indians."

" Well, I expect we are all going to be murdered;
I do. I feel as if I was murdered now."

" Who is going to murder us ? "

" Why, the Indians, — these skearful, scalping
savages that are down here to the brook now ; and
you've sent your children there, right into the very
jaws of destruction. I don't believe they will ever
come back. They say some king or other has died
in Europe, and that has made war between the
Austrians and Prussians (I believe it's Prussians, —
if it ain't, it's no matter), and the Prussians have
got the French to help them ; and the English, they
say, will take up agin the French, because the English king is a relation to the Germans, and has land

there ; and then of course the Colonies will be
brought in, as they always are, and then the French
will stir up all the Indians in Canada, and the whole
tribe of Eastern Indians; and there will be drafting
men, and calling out the militia, and expeditions to
Canada, and men will have to leave their families
and go to cruel war, and your husband will have to
shoulder his gun, and leave you and these children
and the babe that's yet to be born, and march, and
we shall have a bloody mess of it. We are going to
move into Portland right off to-day; and so I've just
run in a minute to bid you good-by, and must go
right home and pack up. But you will go, — of
course you will ; you won't stay here to be murdered
by the raging savages. When we get there my husband will tell Hugh, and he will come back and take
you off to-morrow. My man didn't want to go, but
I told him I would take the children and start right
off afoot before I would stay to be murdered by the
raging savages ; and if he didn't want to see me dead
and in my coffin, he would go this very day."

While Mrs. Ayres was thus going on, wringing
her hands at every word, Elizabeth sat before her
with her knitting-work, as unconcerned as though
there had not been an Indian in the universe,
patiently waiting for her to get out of breath, which
she did at length, winding up with a sort of groan,
and the inquiry, "Ain't you almost scared to
death?"

"Not a bit of it," replied Elizabeth, who now

coolly proceeded to dissect her neighbor's intelli-
gence. " Where did you get this news ? "

" My man got it in Portland."

" Where did it come from ? "

" I don't know ; but it is just as I tell you."

" Does he believe it himself ? "

"Nobody can tell what he believes; he ain't afraid
of anything."

" Did he read it, or see it posted in any handbill,
or did he only hear it ? "

" I don't know."

" Have the general court or selectmen done anything about it ? "

" I don't know."

" Well, I don't believe a word of it; for, in the
first place, if there was anything in it, Hugh, who is
in Portland, would have known it and been here
before this time. If there was prospect of war with
France, the Governor would know it, and put people
on their guard against the Indians the very first
thing. I suppose there is some trouble brewing in
Europe, that in time may bring on a war, and some
people who have nothing else to do have made a
great story out of it."

" Then you ain't a-going ? "

" Not I ! We've worked too hard to get here to
run away on a rumor."

" Well, I'm sorry for you, and your husband, and
your innocent children. You are a hard-hearted
woman, to feel and talk so lightly at such a time,

when the sword is hanging over us, and the raging
savages are to be let loose upon us."

"I suppose," said Elizabeth, a little provoked by
this accusation, "it is because I am not nervous."

"Well, you will have the worst of it; your children will never come back; they will be killed or
carried to Canada, and sold to the Frenchmans."

"But," said Elizabeth, who sat where she could
look out of the door, "they are coming now, and
one of the 'raging savages' with them."

"Then I'll go! for I've never been brought up
to keep company with Indians;" and thus saying,
Mrs. Ayres flung out of the door in a huff, without
bidding her neighbor good-by, — the very purpose
for which she came.

The "raging savage" was Molly Sockbason, one
of some Passamaquoddies who were camping in the
neighborhood. She had a basket in her hand, and a
pappoose on her shoulders; William had hold of one
side of the basket, while Abigail was striving to
reach the baby's face with a bulrush. Elizabeth,
as she looked upon the party, said aloud, "Well,
Ayres's wife is kind-hearted, and I am sorry to lose
the only woman I could speak to without going a
mile. It was so nice to put my shawl over my head
and run in there. But I pity the man who has such
a wife in an Indian country."

The squaw had brought a fish in the basket, and
wanted, in exchange for it, some thread, which
Elizabeth got her wheel and spun, — coarse and

strong, as the Indians preferred to have it. In the
meantime the squaw, taking her child from her
back, set it upon its board against the logs, while
she watched with great interest the spinning; and
the children, getting some milk in a pewter porringer, fed the child with a spoon. Elizabeth then dis-
missed her visitor with the present of a needle, which
greatly delighted her, the Indians preferring our
needles to their own, which were made of a small
bone found in the deer's foot.

The McLellans now had green peas in abundance,
which were a great addition to their store, and potatoes; but the latter they resolutely abstained from
eating, as they could not pull up a hill without de-
stroying many half-grown ones, and thus diminishing
their winter's stock. About a mile to the south was
a sandy plain, where the fires had destroyed the
growth, and a great abundance of blueberries grew.
To this spot the wild pigeons resorted in great
numbers. Knowing the importance of securing such
a seasonable supply, Elizabeth determined to learn
to use the gun; so, having loaded it, she mounted
the horse with William, and proceeded to the place.
The birds being so numerous that she could scarcely
miss, they returned loaded with game, and continued
this profitable sport as long as the pigeons remained;
after which, Elizabeth, by this time an expert shot,
killed many of the raccoons which were improving
the moonlight nights in eating the corn.

The middle of October was now come, and Hugh

came home to his family. It was a most joyful meeting in all respects. Not only were they full of satisfaction to be once more together, but Hugh brought home the money he had earned, not having had to expend a dollar for the support of his family, and finding them better off for provision than they had ever been before, with a noble crop all ready for harvesting. But he had neither barn, cellar, nor garret in which to store his crop, nor cart to haul it on. He at once made a sled for the horse, on which, by light loads, he dragged home his harvest. He then made a crib of logs for his corn, and, digging a pit in the ground below the reach of frost, he put his potatoes there, covering them with timber, over which he put earth, and leaving an entrance in one end, which he carefully covered with brush and waste, that it might be both well protected and easy of access in winter.

In the course of the summer, Elizabeth, going through the woods, and finding that there was to be great abundance of beech-nuts and acorns, bought a pig, which lived very well upon grass and the roots he found in the woods, till the frosts, in the fall, caused the beech-nuts and the acorns to drop, when he became fat, and fit for the knife, without any other feeding.

Elizabeth received with heartfelt satisfaction the well-earned praises of her husband for her excellent management during his absence, and they had many a pleasant talk around the fire in respect to the expedients she had resorted to in order to procure food for the family without drawing on his wages, while Hugh laughed heartily at her exploits in shooting.

Hugh could now look fairly forward to an unbroken winter of work at home, and he improved his time to the utmost. Having at command some ready money, he bought a grindstone, of which, it will be remembered, he stood much in need. He then cleared a road from the southeast part of his land to an old mast-path that ran to the county road at Stroudwater, and cut spars and logs, and made his sleds; and then, in the latter part of the winter, went to Saco, and engaged his brother James and the Pattersons (into whose family James married) to help him haul. They came with their cattle, built a camp in the woods, and hauled till spring, while he continued cutting; and when the warm weather put an end to logging, he found himself better off than he had ever been before in his life, and at liberty to do what he loved best of all, — give himself to farming, without hiring out to work.

There was one man who had watched the progress of Hugh and Elizabeth with great interest, and conceived for them a sincere affection, which was as warmly returned, — Captain Phinney; and he now came down to congratulate them on their good fortune, and spent a sociable evening with them. Hugh, according to the usage of that day, wished to offer him some spirit; but the only metal article they pos-

sessed was one pewter porringer, while they had not
a cup or a tumbler, being all obliged to drink from
the same dish. At supper they had neither wheat-
bread, nor butter, nor tea, nor coffee to offer their
friend, but only pea-soup with pork boiled in it, and
potatoes, and milk to drink, and a corn-cake baked
on a board before the fire. But, for all that, Captain
Phinney told his wife when he came home, that, as
sure as Hugh McLellan lived, he would be a rich
man, and ought to be, and that his wife was equal
to him.

Hugh next burnt over the ground he had cleared
in June, and planted a much larger field of corn than
before. The piece he planted the last year was of
no use for tillage, as it was too full of stumps and
roots to be ploughed, and, besides, neither oxen nor
plough could be had. Only the burnt land, where
the sod was destroyed, and which was full of ashes,
was available.

"Well," said Elizabeth, who always looked at the
advantages rather than the disadvantages of their
situation, "if we were in Ireland now, poor as we
are, without cattle to plough the ground, or manure
to put upon it, and somebody would give us the use
of a piece of land, it would not be worth taking;
while here, (blessed be God!) with nothing but an
axe, a sharp stake, and a firebrand, a poor man can
raise bread for his family."

As Hugh could cut abundance of wild hay in the
woods, he bought half a dozen sheep, and, making a

7

pasture of the land planted before, turned them into
it, together with the cow ; and the grass which came
up there, with the sprouts from the stumps, gave
them a good living.   In order to avoid the great labor of going so far to mill, he dug out a large rock-
maple log for a mortar, and made a pestle, and tied
a rope to the top of it and fastened it to the limb of
a tree, the spring of which helped to lift the pestle,
which was the hardest part of the work.   Part of
the flour was fine enough for bread, and the rest
they boiled and ate with peas and beans.   They had
now a good prospect for a crop, but in the meantime their scanty supply of corn was so nearly gone,
that they had bread but twice a week, and lived
principally on pea-broth and game, with milk.   But
the Indians made game scarce, and the time spent
in hunting interfered seriously with the labor absolutely necessary for the crops.   Often, while getting
hay, they could have no breakfast till Hugh shot a
partridge, or William caught a fish in the brook.   It
is true they had a little money, and might have
bought corn ; but they were hoarding this to purchase a yoke of cattle and farming tools : therefore
they endured with Spartan fortitude the hardship
of short living and scanty clothing, and in the autumn
they succeeded in their purpose.   Hugh, leaving his
wife and William to get in the harvest with the
horse, went to Saco, where he worked for a month,
and returned, bringing with him a yoke of oxen,
large for that day, and broken to work in the woods.

Great was the rejoicing when the cattle came, and Mrs. McLellan said that nothing they afterwards attained ever caused such general delight. Ever after that memorable day, and when they could count their cattle by scores, they always had in the herd a Star and Golding ; and it was said that Uncle Billy, no matter what his oxen's names were, always called them, when he drove, Star and Golding. Hugh said, getting that yoke of cattle seemed to be the turn of his fortune ; that he then had something to work with, and everything seemed to go easier afterwards, though the purchase of them brought him down again to the last dollar.

As he had now cattle, he determined to erect a better dwelling than the old rotten camp, where the snakes lived in the logs and ran over the floor. In anticipation he had peeled some hemlock-bark for the roof in June. Had it been winter, he might at once have hauled logs to the mill and got boards and plank in abundance ; but there was no road passable for wheels. But he wanted to get out of the old camp before another winter, and thus was compelled to make the best of his circumstances. And, after all, the house was a great improvement upon the old camp. The walls of the camp were built of round logs, these were of hewn timber ; the chinks between the logs in the camp were large enough to run your arm through, and were stuffed with moss and clay ; but the timber of the house was hewn to a " proud " edge, and dovetailed together at the ends, and it was as tight as a churn. The camp had no floor, but this had a floor of hewn timber; the walls of the camp were but three logs high, and had settled by decay, so that you could only stand erect in the middle (and a good part of the middle was taken up by the fire), while this was ten feet high, with a chamber, the floor of which was also laid with hewn timber. The camp had but one room, no window, a hole in the roof for a chimney, no oven, so that the bread was baked in the ashes, covered with an iron pot, or on a stone at the fire, while the pot hung by a chain from a pole laid on two crotches; the house had three rooms below, with partitions of bark, and blankets hung up for doors, a fireplace and oven of stone laid in clay mortar, and a chimney made of sticks of split wood, laid *cob*-fashion and plastered inside and out with clay to keep them from catching fire, with a crane to hang the pot on. The roof was covered with hemlock-bark, lapped and nailed as shingles are, and perfectly tight; and there were windows with storm shutters, and two with squares of oiled paper instead of glass. As there was a general apprehension of trouble with the Indians, the windows were made small, and the door was of oak timber with iron hinges, and with a wooden latch on the inside, having a string to lift the latch from the outside; and when the string was pulled in and the bars put up, it would have been no easy matter to force an entrance. The house being built of such thick stuff, and sheltered by the woods on the north and west, with brush piled up around it, into which the snow drifted in the winter, their great fires rendered it perfectly comfortable in the coldest weather.

Into the great kitchen, which extended the whole length of the house, and, after the confinement of the camp, seemed a king's palace, Elizabeth moved with great glee. She instantly set off for Portland, and brought home her loom, which, having no room to set it up in the camp, she had left at Jeanie Miller's; indeed, the camp was so low that she could only spin on the large wheel when the fire was cold, and after the children had gone to bed. In the summer-time she had been wont to take the wheel outdoors under the shade of the trees, and, putting the baby in a blanket, fasten it to the branch of a beech, where it swung in the wind, while she would spin and sing to it, or, taking hold of the branch, would gently sway it up and down, and rock it to sleep; sometimes she would fasten a string to it, by pulling which the children could rock it, or Abigail would sit on the grass and knit and rock the baby. But she had now ample room in the corner of the large kitchen for her loom, wheels, and all her other things. In the opposite end of the kitchen was a log with notches cut in it for steps, up which the children clambered to bed. In the camp they had slept on the ground; but Hugh now hewed out some birch joists, and planed them, and made bedsteads for both parents and children; Elizabeth wove ticks and stuffed them with beech-leaves, which made excellent beds.

These different matters occupied them till snow came ; Hugh then went into the woods, and, hiring another yoke of cattle to go with his, and putting the horse with them, he spent the winter in hauling spars and logs.

For the next two years he continued to clear land, logging in the winter, and gradually bettering his condition. He had now four oxen, hens, hogs, sheep, two cows, and a heifer that he was raising. He had corn and wheat, potatoes, turnips, and cabbages, for he could now plough his land. He also bought pewter plates, and iron spoons, and knives and forks, and they had coffee on Sabbath mornings. They also had flax and wool, and they were better clothed, for they raised all they lived on ; and his winter's logging brought him ready money.

William was now eleven years old, very large for his age, and began to manifest a most wonderful aptitude for hunting and shooting, every spare moment being spent in this manner. Children reared in hardship develop early, and his growth in this direction was greatly hastened by his constant intercourse with the Indian children. The Indians take great pains to instruct their children in the arts of the chase, upon which their existence depends, and put weapons adapted to their age into their hands the moment they are capable of using them. In all these instructions William shared. The older Indians, pleased with his preference for their company and pursuits, made him bows and arrows, some blunt

at the point, and others headed with flint, and
taught him how to use them, predicting that he
would be a great warrior. He practised incessantly
with the Indian children till he could kill with his
arrows squirrels, rabbits, skunks, and even porcupines. He persuaded his father to put a handle into
the old tomahawk which he had found so long since
in the camp; and sticking it into his belt, with his
bow and a wooden knife and an eagle's feather, he
marched through the woods, imagining himself
Bloody Hand, or Leaping Panther, or some other
great brave of whom he had heard. His uncle James,
coming over from Saco to pay them a visit, asked
William, as the family were seated after supper before the door, to let them see how well he could
shoot. They looked on in astonishment to see him
knock a bumble-bee off a thistle with a blunt arrow
at forty yards, and a squirrel from the top of a beech
with a sharp-pointed one. His uncle declared that
such a talent for shooting ought to be encouraged,
especially in such times as those when it might come
into play; and said that he had a light gun he would
give him when he was a few months older. Nothing
could have given William greater pleasure than this,
and he looked eagerly forward to the time when he
should receive it.

Hitherto, Hugh had limited his lumbering operations to getting out spars for merchantmen, and
logs to be manufactured into boards and planks,
great quantities of which were shipped from Portland

to Europe and the West Indies. But as he had now
cattle of his own and provisions for his family, he
determined to cut and haul the masts for the king's
ships, great numbers of which he had upon his land,
of the largest size and the best quality.

A few words of explanation may here be necessary. Though Portland was now rapidly rising from
its ashes, and ships were built, and there was a large
export trade, and it had been settled a hundred years
before, yet so often had it been laid in ashes, and its
inhabitants driven off or destroyed by the savages,
that all this period had been occupied in carrying
settlements nine miles from the sea-coast. But it
must not therefore be concluded that these forests
had not been penetrated by white men, and their
riches known and prized. There was but little danger in lumbering compared with settling, — merely
going into the woods for a short time to cut and haul
timber, with a body of hardy men, unincumbered
by women or children, all in a body, armed to the
teeth, and as ready to fight as to eat. There was
also less danger in lumbering, because it was pursued only in the winter, when the Indians left the
coast to hunt farther back in the country. Hence
there were many early logging-roads cut through
the woods in various directions, which, suitable for
lumbering in the winter, when the snow made
all level, were impassable in summer, except on
foot or horseback. One of these roads, now much
overgrown, it having been disused since the Indian

troubles in 1722, ran near Hugh's lot. This road he cut out, and extended it to a swale where some masts of great size grew, one of which, as Grannie declared, was so big that a yoke of cattle were turned around upon the stump without stepping off. This tree stood near where a carpet-factory has since been built.

Although the trees marked with the broad arrow could not be appropriated by the owner of the soil to his own use, the English government paid him a bounty, and, if he saw fit to cut and haul them, liberal pay for his labor. The government found its account in this, for the masts were more valuable than those obtained from Sweden or Norway, and the bounty was an encouragement to the settlers to preserve them, even if they did no more. For though the authorities could prevent the owner of the soil from making use of them, and punish him if he did, detection was difficult, and it could not prevent him from clearing the land around them, when the wind would tear them up by the roots, or from setting a fire that would very likely kill them in burning his other land. Indeed, they were in constant danger from the fires running through the woods, from lightning and tempest, and the commissioners were always ready to employ the settlers to cut them. Still the market never was overstocked. The trees were of immense size, many more than five feet in diameter, very difficult to handle and to haul with the small cattle then reared; and while

the job also required some outlay of money, the
inhabitants were poor and scattered; and thus
thousands of trees marked with the broad arrow
stood for half a century in the forests, against which
no axe was uplifted. But the inducements for
enterprise were great; money was scarce, lumber
of all kinds brought money, and when the masts
were at the ship's tackles the cash was ready. Hugh
felt himself equal to the task, and with him to
decide was to execute. All through the first of the
winter he was in the woods from dawn of day till
the stars appeared in the sky, and sometimes by
moonlight or firelight in the evening. But they
were happy days, — the happiest of his life; he
had a frame of iron, and labor was a delight; every
blow struck was for himself, his children, and his
homestead. Stripped to the waist, his sinewy arms
bare to the elbow, and the perspiration standing in
drops upon his face, the blows fell fast and heavy,
till the enormous column, tottering and trembling
for a moment, fell to the ground, flinging the broken
branches high in the air, and with a noise like
distant thunder. Nor was his work always solitary:
sometimes of a pleasant afternoon Elizabeth would
come down, and, sitting on a root in the sun, knit
her stocking, sometimes a party of Indians on their
way to Portland or Saco would sit down by his fire,
eagerly accepting the pipe he offered, and, as they
smoked in silence, gaze evidently with dissatisfac-
tion upon the havoc he was making in the forest,

A Pleasant Afternoon in the Woods.   Page 106.

which was rapidly diminishing the game, and with it their means of living. Then, in sullen dignity wrapping their blankets around them, they would say: "White man cut much trees. Much trees, much moose, much bear; no trees, no moose, no bear, — Indian starve." No wonder they thus felt; for many years the whites had been confined to a little rim of settlements along the coast, and often had been entirely driven out and their dwellings burnt. At intervals they had penetrated a few miles, and cut a few masts and logs; but now, as the Indians travelled, they passed the mills of Colonel Gorham, on the Presumpscot, and the clearing of Captain Phinney, who had now turned many acres of forest into cultivated fields. Other settlers were building camps, and the sound of falling trees was heard on every side. A shade of anxiety would cross Hugh's face while he followed with his eye their forms stalking away with noiseless tread, for he saw that his work did not please them, that their methods of life and his could by no means go on together, and that the work which put bread into his mouth took it from them.

CHAPTER V.

T HE time had now come for hauling. Hugh,
during his residence at Falmouth and Saco,
had established a character for industry, integrity,
and good judgment, by which and the efforts of his
brother James and his cousin Bryce he obtained men
and teams, who, as the value of the masts was fixed
and the pay sure, agreed to help him " on shares."
Hugh improved the first snow that fell by hauling
some logs to the mill at Sacarappa, where they were
sawed into boards and plank.   With these he made
a long table, and some settles to place before the fire,
with backs as high as the top of a person's head, to
break off the drafts of wind that went up the great
chimney.   He also made some benches as long as the
table, one for each side, and supplied doors between
the rooms instead of blankets, and board partitions
in lieu of hemlock bark.   But he was so anxious to
get the masts cut before the neighbors came to help
him, that he worked in the woods through all the
storms, and made his doors, settles, and benches in

the evenings; and as they had no candles, when he had to work away from the fire-light William held some splinters of pitch-wood, which answer very well for candles.

Great was the excitement in that lonely household, the members of which but seldom saw a white face beyond the circle of their own family, when at noon of the appointed day there came ten men, with twenty oxen, bringing their hay and provisions on sleds. All was now bustle both in doors and out. Elizabeth had been up long before day, and had heated the ovens and baked beans, and made Indian puddings, and boiled beef and pork and cabbages, for they now had abundance.

" We certainly ought to be thankful," said she to her husband, as she looked over the table to see if all was in order, " that we can set such a table as this, and nearly everything on it from our own land."

" It is all from our own land," he replied; " for though we bought the beef, our timber paid for it, and I rather think that will be the easiest way to get all the provision. But only see what it is to have oxen; for, as the blessed Book says, 'much increase is by the strength of the ox;' and we certainly ought not to forget old Star and Golding. If it were not for them, we should not have a table to eat from."

The children had been up ever since daybreak, aroused by the crackling of the fire in the oven, and Abigail was not half dressed, which her mother had

been too busy and excited herself to notice. They
kept right at their mother's heels, scrutinizing every
motion, except when they were sent to bring in
wood or water. It was a great day to them. They
had never seen so many people together in their
lives as would be at their house to dine that day,
and it was only a few months since they had first
seen an ox, so that the novelty of the sight had
hardly worn off. They could not be satisfied with
looking at and feeling of the new pewter plates
shining like silver, which were now brought out for
the first time, the great pewter platters and porringers, the brown earthen drinking-mugs, and the
cranberries, stewed and sweetened with molasses,
which Elizabeth had got of the Indians, — for
nobody else knew where they grew. All these
things were new to them, for they had been used to
see on the table only wooden plates and drinking-
vessels, and wooden or horn spoons. When at length
they heard the shouts of the teamsters in the distance, coming slowly, as they with difficulty urged
their weary cattle through the deep snow, which had
not yet been broken, they rushed bareheaded from
the house, in an ecstasy of happiness and wonder
that is beyond all description. Hugh's cattle, and
even the horse, shared in the general excitement;
the horse whinnied, the oxen bellowed, and the calf
ran in between the strange cattle, and astride of the
chains, and between the bars of the sleds, and cut
up all kinds of antics. The oxen were chained to

trees and fed, but, worn out with their journey, —
for they had been out all night, — they dropped
down in the snow and refused to eat. The men,
scarcely less weary, passed into the great kitchen,
where a blazing fire was roaring in the huge fireplace, and the bountiful table spread. Hugh had
stationed himself by the door with a pailful of New
England rum and water sweetened, and as they
came in gave each one a drink, after which all
took their seats at the table, where, after the grace,
Hugh and his wife and William waited upon them.

The contents of the great pewter platters disappeared with great celerity before the hungry guests
who had been wading all night in the deep snow,
and had not broken their fast since the day before.
Their hunger being at length appeased, they drew
up around the great fire, and dried their wet clothes,
and thawed their frozen shoes and leggings, and
rested an hour or so.

Refreshed by the hearty meal, the warmth, and
the short rest, they took their axes and proceeded to
a growth of small pines within a short distance of
the house. The keen blades, swung in practised
hands, flashed in the air, the woods rang with the
din of blows, and soon the long, slim trees lay widely
prostrate. Some now began to cut them into appro-
priate lengths, while others notched and rolled them
up ; and in an incredibly short time a rude hovel
rose where a few hours before had been the dense
forest. A floor was now laid with poles, — pun-

cheons, as they termed them, — which Hugh, who
was most skilful with the broadaxe, had been hewing
on one side, — all which the time permitted. The
stanchions for tying the cattle were now put in,
which had been brought all made, and the neck
bows; a roof of brush was then put on, the hay put
in, and just as the twilight came on the tired oxen
were released from the yoke and placed in their new
quarters.

In addition to the government timber, Hugh had
cut a lot of smaller spars, for which there was always
a ready market. The royal timber was also of different sizes; the masts were immense sticks, three
feet in diameter after they were hewn, and more
than a hundred feet in length; the bowsprits were
larger, but much shorter, while the yards were
smaller still. The party had in the first place to
break the road with empty sleds, it being all the
oxen could do to get through the deep snow; then
they took light loads of the small spars, which they
continued to haul for some days, — in the meantime carefully examining the road, cutting off all
roots and limbs that projected into it, putting poles
in all the soft places, and treading down the snow
into them that it might freeze, and make a hard
road, and making the necessary bridges in the gullies, till all the way was as hard and smooth as
glass. Then they put on a bowsprit to try, which
from its different shape was much less difficult to
haul than a mast. As the road bore this without

HAULING TIMBER.   Page 113

" slumping," they now loaded one of the large masts. This was very exciting work, and especially to the children and Elizabeth, who looked on.

Men were stationed by the middle cattle to keep them from getting down, or getting the chain over their backs in crossing the gullies and knolls; for they were sometimes hung up by the neck for a moment, and a chain straightened over a creature's back would break it instantly. Men were also stationed by the sled with ropes to keep it from turning bottom up. But when the great mass moved off at the word of command, the sled creaking and groaning under the weight, the drivers shouting, and the oxen exerting themselves to the utmost, Captain Phinney took off his hat and gave a cheer for the first mast cut and hauled in the town of Gorham since it had received that name; in which all joined, the shrill screams of the children, who wellnigh split their throats in striving to perform their parts, predominating over the rest.

They sometimes took a day or two and beat up the quarters of a bear, or hunted moose upon the crust, to help out their provisions; and thus they went on successfully, getting out mast after mast, without accident to man or beast, till the advent of spring put an end to their work.

When they came to settle up the winter's labor and divide the proceeds, Hugh found himself in possession of more money than he had ever seen before in his life. Encouraged by this, he determined

8

to devote his whole attention to the occupation which he had found so profitable.

But though successful, he received a lesson which he never forgot, since he and his family were brought nearer to starvation than ever before. He hired two hands, and went to cutting masts for the next win-ter's work, peeling the bark off to keep the worms from spoiling them. When haying-time came, he mowed all the wild grass he could find in the natural meadows and old beaver-dams and stacked it, making abundant provision for his cattle in the winter. Then, not having planted a hill of corn, and only a few potatoes and peas, he set himself to cutting masts, intending to buy his bread, and give his whole mind and time to lumbering. By the middle of November he had a great number of masts and other lumber ready to haul on the first snows.

But now occurred a misfortune, which it is not surprising an emigrant and a stranger in the country should not have foreseen, — especially as hundreds born in the country, and better advised, were in the same condition. Silver and gold were at that time scarce, and almost all trade was by barter. To this lumbering was an exception, and offered a direct means of getting hard money, whence followed a universal neglect of farming in Maine. The result of which, in turn, was a great scarcity of breadstuff. As this was procured from the Carolinas and other parts of the country by small vessels, in the winters, when vessels could not get in to the coast, the scarcity at times amounted to a famine, and became especially severe at such times with those outlying settlers who were separated by wide and almost impassable woods from any place where corn could be procured. The last time that the team went down with a mast, Hugh had bought and hauled home corn enough to have lasted him, under ordinary circumstances, till February. But as he had neglected hunting altogether that he might cut masts, he had little meat, and so consumed more corn. He had no harvest to look forward to, and by the middle of November, when his stock was greatly reduced, he found that, as the great body of settlers in Maine had done pretty much like himself, there was scarcely any corn or grain in the whole eastern country, — that the great bulk of the people must, till another year, depend for food upon the uncertain supplies that came by coasters, — and, going to Portland to get an axe, he made the alarming discovery that there was no corn there to be had at any price. In addition to this, as he had determined upon buying his corn, he had kept but one spring pig, and so had but little pork to raise.

"Well, wife," said Hugh, somewhat depressed after telling her the state of things, "I thought if we had money, we could not but get on; and now that we have more money than we ever had in our lives, we are like to starve. It makes me think of a story I have heard about an Arab who was travelling in the desert, and in a starving condition. He espied a bag on the ground, and, hoping it might be bread, picked it up; but it contained only pearls."

"Don't be distrustful, Hugh," replied his wife, whose spirit nothing could depress, "after all that God has brought us through. Look at this nice, comfortable house, and remember that first night in the old camp; and only look at this," — placing a plump and savory-steaming partridge before him, that Billy had shot that morning with his bow and arrow. "Depend upon it, my laddie, it is not those who have money who are going to starve, even in a famine; it was never so in the old country, for they would still find some means to get what little there was."

Encouraged by the cheery tone of his sage coun-sellor, backed by a voracious appetite (for the cold and hungry man had eaten nothing since morning, and had brought an axe and a half-bushel of salt on his back nine miles through the woods), and with his back to the blazing fire, he made short work of the partridge, drank up a platter of hot pea-soup, and finished with sundry thick slices of bread. But when, having satisfied his hunger, he turned round to the great fire, and stretched out his wet feet to the grateful heat, and met the cheerful countenance of his wife, who, too industrious to lose any time, sat knitting on the block in the corner, while in the other corner lay Billy, stretched at full length on the hearth, with his feet to the fire, and he noticed the great bones and sinews of the boy, giving promise of early and efficient partnership in his own toils, — he began to be of his wife's opinion.

"You are better than I am, Elizabeth," said he;
"and I ought to be ashamed of myself, and I am.
God forgive me! We are ungrateful creatures at
the best."

"I have not been travelling all day through the
swamps with a load on my back," said she, "but
sitting here by the warm fire; and we feel down-
hearted when we are tired and hungry. But now
take the good Book, and thank God for all his mer-
cies, for surely they have been many."

Hugh prayed, and was strengthened. They then,
after laying their plans to meet this new emergency,
retired to rest. The result of this matrimonial counsel was soon apparent. The allowance of bread in
the family was diminished, and a whole week spent
in hunting, and the meat dried in the smoke, after
the method of the Indians. Hugh went to Portland
and bought a quantity of pickled and dry fish. A
great quantity of acorns, beech-nuts, ground-nuts,
and lily-roots were gathered and dried and stored
up; these last were to grind with the corn, to make
it hold out longer. As there were a good many
masts cut, a large part of the time was devoted to
hunting, which the coming cold weather and deep
snows would render difficult.

Hugh, now expecting the teams, took some of the
boards which he had obtained during the last winter,
and laid a floor in the chamber above, and all over
the lower part of the house, that it might be warmer
than the timber floor, which was open and rough-

laid, while this was double, planed and jointed, and as tight as a cup. But that which pleased Elizabeth most of all was the procuring of a Dutch oven, — which was a flat-bottomed iron kettle, having an iron cover with a rim around it two inches high. This was put on the fire, and hot coals put on the cover, and thus, with heat both above and below, bread or meat baked nicely, — which saved heating the great oven, and, as the bread baked in half the time it would on a board by the fire, this was a great help in the short, cold winter mornings when so many men were to have their breakfast before light, that they might get the cattle fed, and be in the woods by sunrise.

Hugh now went over the road and removed the trees that had blown down or fallen across it in the summer, and put new poles in all the miry spots, and skids in the hollows. The snow soon came, and with it, much earlier in the season than before, the teams and men. They had made so good a winter's work the year before, that they were eager to begin as soon as possible. All their talk this winter was about the scarcity of corn and grain, for all alike felt the hand of poverty, and all were agreed in opinion that the settlers in the eastern country had made a great mistake in devoting themselves so much to lumbering. Indeed, some of them confessed that, though they had five hundred acres of land, they had not planted a hill of anything, but had spent the entire year (except when they were cutting their hay) in cutting and hauling timber, or rafting it down the rivers, or at work in the mills; and now corn was thirty shillings a bushel, and little to be had at that, the holders keeping it for a higher price, knowing that people must buy or starve. Solemn resolutions were made that, if they escaped starvation this time, they would never be caught doing the like again.

" But the worst of it is," said Patterson, of Saco, " if we go on in this way, we shall not be able to lumber much longer, for we shall have no hay for the oxen, because we burn over the land, and don't plough it, but let it lie, and so it bears no grass, but grows up to fire-weed, and pigeon-weed, and wild-cherry, and all kind of stuff, — the forest over again." Indeed, such was the case to some extent then, for one of the men who was short of hay, and had four oxen, offered Hugh one yoke of them for their keeping, which, as he had abundance of hay, was gladly accepted; for Hugh had formed quite different plans for the next year, in consequence of his bitter experience.

By hunting, grinding acorns and the cobs of the corn together with the kernel, they contrived to make the corn hold out till the hauling season was over, though their meat diet brought on various disorders and eruptions. But when the company was gone, and the bustle and cheerfulness which their presence caused no longer existed, and they were left alone, — with cows almost dry, the deep snows so favorable for the taking of moose and deer diminished, the

bears, raccoons, and beaver leaving their dens, and no
longer to be taken as before, and the children, miss-
ing their milk, beginning to cry for the bread which
could not be given them except in scanty morsels, —
the hearts of the parents grew heavy, and their minds
were filled with gloomy thoughts. As a penance
for the past year's neglect, the father now began to
cut trees for a burn; but his arm, enfeebled by
hunger, struck but feeble blows; still he persevered,
and performed about half his usual task. In this
extremity they resorted to various expedients; ma-
ple-sugar was boiled with milk and roots, and eaten
to allay the cravings of hunger. Many a time did
Hugh drop his axe, and, falling on his knees in the
lonely forest, plead with Heaven for aid, rising to
return with renewed courage to his labor.

At this period of distress an Indian, who had been
out hunting without success, (belonging to a party
who had camped at Sebago Pond,) entered the
house, evidently faint and weary, and, approaching
Elizabeth, said, "Indian hungry." She, without a
moment's hesitation, gave him a portion of her
scanty allowance, although she was then boiling
lily-roots for the children's dinner, together with
elm-bark and hazel-nuts. She then spread a blanket for him by the fire, and he lay down to sleep.
Arising completely refreshed, he pursued his journey,
departing without a word of acknowledgment.

In four days from this time the same Indian came,
and, laying on the table a porcupine's skin filled

with corn, and the hind leg of a beaver, said, "Squaw have big heart; she have little, she feed Indian. Indian he have big heart too; he feed squaw." His keen eye, well read in the signs of hunger, had detected its ravages in the faces of the mother and children, and he hastened to repay the kindness.

William, who had gone to Saco to try to purchase some corn, now returned with only a peck, with the gun his uncle had promised him, and a dog, — a puppy of a large and excellent breed; and it would be difficult to tell which he was the most delighted with, the dog or the gun.

"Why, William McLellan!" exclaimed Elizabeth, when she saw this unwelcome addition to their family. "Have we not hungry mouths enough to fill now, that you must needs bring this good-for-nothing puppy to eat us out of house and home? I thought you had more sense, William."

"O mother," he replied, "the dog will help fill our mouths, instead of taking anything out of them;" and so indeed it proved, for he not only aided essentially in the support of the family, but finally became the means of saving their lives, and the mother often had occasion to change her hasty conclusion.

William spent the remainder of the day in cleaning his gun, and running bullets to fit it, in a mould which his uncle had also given him. The next morning early he started with the dog for the woods, and in two hours came back with three raccoons.

" Why, Will," said his mother, overjoyed, for it
was long since they had procured any meat, "how
did you get all these so quick ? "

" *I* didn't get them," said he, rejoiced to vindicate
his dog's character ; " I never should have got 'em :
the dog got 'em. They were all coiled up round the
body of a spruce, right at the buts of the limbs, —
O, just as snug ! — and I might have gone under the
tree a hundred times without seeing them, they were
so near the color of the bark ; but Bose scented
them, and began to bark, — you don't know how he
did bark, — he barked *awful*, and began to scratch,
and stand up on his hind legs, and put his fore paws
against the tree, and then I saw 'em."

A few days after, Bose treed some partridges,
which Billy shot and brought home ; and he found
the holes of raccoons and woodchucks in hollow
trees and logs ; and William cut them out, and the
dog shook them till he killed them.

At length, one day when his father was away,
William came to his mother in great excitement.
The dog had found a bear in a den.

" How do you know there is but one ? " said his
mother.

" Because I saw him go in."

Here was a great temptation. The weather was
cold enough for the meat to keep a long time, and,
as they were without pork, the fat was a great item
to the mother in her cookery, and the skin was valuable to sell, or for clothing. Elizabeth reflected

some moments while the son eagerly watched his mother's face to anticipate her decision ; finally, to his great delight, she said, " William, we must have that bear. Providence has put him in our way, and it seems to be our duty. We shall certainly be protected in doing our duty."

" It wasn't Providence, ma'am, it was Bose," cried Billy ; " he drove him into the den."

" Well, it was Providence that sent us Bose, Billy."

Thus doubly fortified by hunger and a sense of duty, after William had loaded the guns they sallied forth.

" Mother," said Billy, " it's better that your gun should be empty than mine. I'll start him out, and you fire."

He tried by thumping on the den, which was under a windfall where two trees had blown down together, to make the brute come out; but the bear, which, as they afterwards found, had been hunted before, only growled and refused to come.

" You disobliging old scamp," said Billy, "*I'*ll make you come, you see if I don't ; " and, going to the house for a firebrand, he set the den on fire. No sooner had the smoke begun to penetrate the den, than the bear began to sneeze, and soon came out, receiving the contents of Elizabeth's gun in his face and eyes.

William, thus early manifesting the cool judgment that distinguished him in after life, had loaded his

mother's gun with shot, knowing that the scattering
would do much to make up for the inaccuracy of
aim, and would blind and bother the bear, and afford
him and the dog a better opportunity to deal with
him.   But confident in the sureness of his own aim,
he had loaded his gun with two balls.   While the
bear, half blind and mad with pain, hesitated a moment, the dog seized him behind, and, rising on his
hind legs to confront the dog, he received William's
fire, who, resting his gun over the windfall, took
deliberate aim, and shot him dead.

" Didn't Bose do well, mother ? " said William.

" I think you did well, my boy ; you shot him,"
replied she.

" But I never could have shot him so slick, if
Bose hadn't taken hold of him behind ; that stopped
him, and I had a chance for a rest, and couldn't help
hitting him."

They now took the oxen and sled to haul the
carcass to the house ; but the cattle would not go
near the brute, and finally got away from them, and,
snorting and trembling, ran home.   So they skinned
and cut the bear up in the woods, and took it home
on the back of the horse, which, accustomed to ad-
ventures, was not a bit afraid of a dead bear.   Ever
after this Bose had a warm place by the fire, and
shared with the family the provisions he contributed
in so great a degree to procure.

Bose often went hunting on his own account, and
would dig out and bring home animals, and then

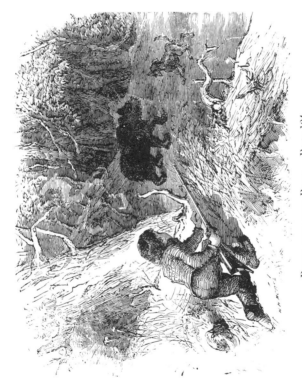

PILLY AND THE BEAR.   Page 124.

cover them up in the ground, to eat at his leisure. If he found an animal that he could not get at, he would come home and by signs invite his master to follow him to the place. He had an unconquerable antipathy to Indians. He would scent them at a great distance, and it was necessary to tie him up when they were about, to keep him from tearing the Indian children to pieces, and the Indians from shooting him. The moment he scented one at a distance he would begin to growl, and the hair on his back would rise up.

The frost was soon out, and the land which Hugh had first cleared was in a state to plough, the stumps and roots being tender with decay. He had now, with his own cattle and those he had taken to winter, a powerful team, and he hired help, and broke up a large piece of ground. He then took the ends of the ears of corn which were not fit to plant, and ground them together with the cob and some acorns, — which was the last of their corn, although it had been husbanded with the greatest care, and they had been on allowance for four months. But while the last baking was in the oven, he heard from his brother at Saco that a vessel had come in with corn, that the civil authorities were compelling the owners to sell it in small lots and at a moderate price, and that three bushels had been secured for him. This good news was brought by John Cutts, one of the men who worked with him in the winter, — the same man who let him have the oxen, and who had now come for his cattle, bringing half a bushel of the corn on his back.

"I knew you were short as you could be," said John, "and thought I would make you glad to see me."

They were indeed glad to see him, and as blessings or troubles rarely come single, it was announced that one of the cows had calved, and the children were jubilant with the prospect of milk. A pleasant evening was that, and bear-meat tasted delicious now there was bread to go with it. A mighty corn-loaf was baked, and the other batch, half baked, was taken from the oven and thrown away.

As there were no newspapers, all news was communicated by word of mouth, and John informed them of all that had occurred during the winter, — who had died, who had been married, the news from England, the sufferings of the people for want of bread, and the doings of the Great and General Court in Boston, — and so the evening passed pleasantly away.

The next morning Hugh set out for Saco to get his corn, and then he heard that a vessel had arrived at Portland with four thousand bushels more. The fact was, that these vessels had been detained off the coast many weeks by northerly winds, and then came in together. After resting a day he went to Portland, and brought home ten bushels more and some pork. Hugh thought the face of nature never looked so beautiful as on that day. He whis-

tled, he sang " The Battle of the Boyne Water."
He smiled to himself as he reflected upon the happiness the provisions he was carrying would occasion
in his family, nor did he forget to lift up his heart
in gratitude to God, the author of all his blessings.

Ere long it was the 10th of May, and the leaves
on the white oak were as big as a mouse's ear, —
the Indian sign that the time was near for planting
corn. Hugh, taught by past experience, put in all
the seed-corn he then had (as the corn he procured
at Saco and Portland was southern corn and not
fit for planting), and a large piece of potatoes, which
were not generally raised at that time, together with
wheat, beans, and peas ; he then made his burn,
and planted corn there. During the whole summer
he gave his attention to the cultivation of the soil,
and again bought fowls and hogs, as they had been
obliged to eat up all theirs. William went to Saco,
and obtained ducks' and turkeys' eggs, and set them
under hens ; and the ducks lived finely in the brook,
which abounded in frogs upon which they fed.

When autumn came round they had the satisfaction of looking upon fields rich with harvest. The
coons dared not trouble the corn, for Bose shook
some of them to pieces ; and that, and his barking
in the nights, frightened away the rest. Hugh
filled his crib with ears of sound corn, and festoons
of it were hung up all around the kitchen, much
more than he needed for his family. They had pork
and milk and eggs in abundance, with a noble crop

of wheat, for this was before the day of the Hessian fly. Since he had no barn-floor to thresh it on, he threshed it upon boards laid on the ground.

Hugh had now a remarkable illustration of the wisdom of not neglecting the cultivation of the soil in order to lumber. The great majority did not lay to heart the bitter experience of the last year ; but, unable to resist the fascination of the woods, so soon as the vessels came with corn, forgot all their past sufferings. Therefore, though there was no famine, yet corn bore so high a price that Hugh with the proceeds of the corn he sold was enabled to hire help enough to cut and get out as many masts as he did the year before, when he neglected everything for lumbering, and almost starved in the winter beside. When the teams came again to commence lumbering, Hugh was able to receive them in even better style than at first, and had constructed bunks like those in a vessel, so that the men slept upstairs, and lay till breakfast-time (except the one who got up to feed the cattle), and thus were not in the kitchen and in the way when Elizabeth was getting her breakfast.

Next came the spring of 1744, and to the great joy of the McLellans, other settlers began to move into their vicinity. For two years people had been coming in, but not near them ; yet it had been of the utmost advantage, as it had enabled them to have the preaching of the Gospel, the want of which they had felt to be one of their greatest deprivations ;

and they had just now had six months' preaching. " I should be so glad," said Hugh sometimes to his wife, " to have a near neighbor ; when I am chopping, to hear the sound of somebody's axe beside my own. I often think Bose would like to have some other dog to bark at, instead of having always to bark at the moon, or hold a concert with the wolves and foxes."

" I am sure I should," said Elizabeth ; " I should like to have some woman that I could run in and see, and ask about anything I am doing. You know a woman's work is different from a man's. Men ask each other about their work, and take lots of comfort talking about it with one another, and so women do just the same. Often, when I am making a gown for Abigail, or something for William, or putting a piece in the loom, or coloring something, I think if I only had somebody to whom I could say, ' How would you do this ? ' or ' How does this set ? ' And then about cooking, — people do things so differently. I have nobody to ask but you, and it is plain to be seen that you don't know or care ; but if it was a woman, — especially a woman who had children, — it would be different. I am sure I miss Mrs. Ayres ; she was a great deal better than no neighbor, though she was a poor rickety creature, and afraid of her own shadow."

9

CHAPTER VI.

INDIAN PLAYFELLOWS.

WE ought to have schools," said Elizabeth one day; "our children will be savages; and I do want some playmates for them other than Indians. William is more than half Indian now; he talks Indian, struts about with a knife and tomahawk, and all he cares about is hunting. Since he shot the bear, the old Indians tell him he will be a great chief, and sometimes I fear he will go off with them. The other day he had a whole parcel of paint, — going, as he said, on the war-path. I suppose the Indian children put it into his head."

But they were now to have their wishes gratified. One pleasant afternoon Captain Phinney came down with his wife to supper, and, as there was a moon, they were persuaded to spend the evening. Elizabeth had been long desirous of having them as guests, not merely because she had a great affection and respect for them, but because she was now able to entertain them well, and, if the truth must be told, that she might show her new house and dishes.

She could now set on the spirit in a pewter tankard scoured as bright as silver, and with it pewter porringers to drink from; she could offer also in earthen cups some tea, which was then a great luxury, drank only two or three times a year, — at Thanksgiving, and when the minister came. After supper Hugh took the company to see his stock, four large oxen and three cows, with half a dozen sheep and pigs. Then he showed his wheat in a chamber, and, in a lower room parted off from the kitchen, his carpenter's bench and tools, and a shoe-maker's bench covered with moose-hide, on which were awls and lasts and pincers that he had brought from Ireland. Finally he uncovered the potatoes, the sight of which greatly astonished and pleased them. "Why," said the Captain, "I had no idea there were any potatoes raised near here. Where did you get the seed?"

Hugh then told them that, when he repaired the vessel at York, he found some that a passenger had left in one of the berths, and, having no land, gave them to his brother James; but when he came to this place he had taken the seed again and planted it.

Elizabeth had also her treasures to show: butter that she had put down in the summer, a piece of thick cloth that she had woven for breeches and jackets, table-linen and towels, figured and bleached as white as snow, linen yarn, spun almost as fine as silk, and deer-skins, which she had learned from the

Indians how to dress, and which were as soft as
cloth. The table-linen and the napkins were in
a box of birch-bark, worked with differently colored
porcupine-quills, blue, red, and yellow. "Look at
this," said she, taking from the box a beautiful
table-cloth which Hugh's mother had woven and
given to her at their marriage; "how handsome
this is! and yet the figures on this box, worked by
the wild savages, are handsomer. I often wonder at
their work when I see their tools."

When they were again seated before the fire,
Captain Phinney said to Mr. McLellan : "I am
astonished when I consider how you have got along
in the world. About two years since I took supper
with you in the old camp; we all had to drink out
of one dish, for you were very, very poor, with
a small family and no help. Now you have a better
house and better stock than I have, more corn and
grain, and almost as much land cleared ; yet I had no
land to pay for, and had two stout boys to help me."

"And when I look back," replied Hugh, "it
appears to me like a dream. I lay it to the good
providence of God, who has blessed the labor of our
hands. I think, however, you are at fault when you
say that I have had no help. A kind Providence
gave me this wife to begin the world with, who has
been more to me than a whole family of boys. Not
only has she done the work of the house, which
other women deem sufficient, and which is all any
man ought to ask, but she has helped me in the

field, has reaped grain, dug potatoes, pulled flax, and got in a whole harvest when I was away, and has even cut down trees and done many other things which I never would have permitted her to do had it not been for my extreme poverty. She has aided me by counsel, and encouraged me when I felt worn out and depressed. William also, young as he is, has been a great help in the way of obtaining provisions. I do not know how we could have got through the last winter, had it not been for him and his dog."

Captain Phinney having succeeded in drawing out his favorite, William, to tell the story of the bear, the company laughed heartily when he came to his mother's saying that it was their duty to kill it, and Mrs. Phinney doubted very much whether she should have considered it her duty to make such an exertion.

"But, William," said the Captain, when the story was finished, "you give nearly all the credit to Bose. Now it is Bose's *nature* to clinch a bear; I might say yours too, for you have come to be almost an Indian. It seems to me that your mother was the leader, after all, and ought to have the most credit."

"I thought everybody knew what mother is," said Billy; "for a good many times father has said to me in the woods, 'William, help your mother all you can when I am away, for there is not such another mother in the world.' But I thought you didn't know about Bose, and I wanted you should."

Elizabeth blushed at this incidental proof of her husband's appreciation, and said : "I never was much used to dogs, and when William brought this one home I felt sorry and provoked, as we had then so little to eat for ourselves. But I have been astonished to find how valuable a dog is in a new settlement, as a help in hunting, and a safeguard too. I didn't like to have Abigail play so much with the Indian children, but she had no other playmates ; in the winter she could not go to your house, — it was so far, — and in the summer the bears and wolves were about : but now that we have a dog, he goes with her, and I don't feel concerned. Besides, Bose is good company when my husband is gone."

"But why did you learn to use a gun?" said Mrs. Phinney.

"Necessity," said Elizabeth, smiling, "drove me to that, as it has to many other things, and not any fondness for shooting. Hugh had paid away his last dollar for land, we had a crop in the ground, and he was away working hard to earn money to buy provision to live on till that ripened. We had not an ox, sheep, or plough, and needed money to buy them, and I could not bear to take every cent for food as fast as he earned it, when there was game all around us in the woods. William was then too young to handle a gun, so I determined to learn. Besides, I felt that, if there should be trouble with the Indians, I might be the means of saving the lives of some of my family ; and now that I can shoot, I mean to practise till the Indian troubles are over, or there are more men hereabouts than at present."

"It is a noble resolution," cried Captain Phinney, gazing with undisguised admiration upon the speaker; "and nothing but good can come of it. But this talk of Indians reminds me to tell you the last news, which is, that it is the opinion in high quarters that there will be a general war in Europe on account of the Austrian succession, and it is almost certain that war will be declared by England against France, and then we shall have another Indian war. There are but two courses open to us," continued he. "One is, to build a garrison, in which our families may be secure, and stay by to work our land; the other is, to flee to Saco, or elsewhere, till the war is over. If we remain in our houses, we shall all be cut off; if we build a garrison, the government will furnish us with cannon and a guard of soldiers. There will be time enough to build a garrison after we know that war is declared, but in the meantime we should be making up our minds either to go or stay; and as I know you to be persons of good judgment and resolution, I wish to get your opinions and advice."

"I can speak only for myself," said Hugh. "I am for staying where I am. Here are my property, and all the means of getting bread I have. If a sufficient number will stay to build a garrison, I will stay, be they many or few. But I shall leave all other considerations to my wife ; in such a time the women and children suffer most."

" I," said Elizabeth, " am of the same mind as my husband — I am for staying."

" It is the decision I expected you would come to," said the Captain, " and it is mine likewise. Mosier is also for staying. There are quite a number of us, all able-bodied men, and more are coming to join us. With a good garrison and strict watch, and under the Divine blessing, I hope we may win in any war; it is also possible that all trouble may blow over. But there is another more pleasant matter I wish to speak about. I expect you are going to have a very near neighbor."

" I shall rejoice at that," replied Hugh, " if he proves a good one."

" His name is Watson, and he is the husband of Elizabeth, my eldest daughter. He is going to take up the lot on the ridge west of you, so that your lands will join."

" Have they children ? " said Elizabeth.

" They are young married folks, and have but two. Though it would perhaps come better from some one else, I will say that Eliphalet Watson is an industrious, resolute, God-fearing man, and will be to you a first-rate friend and neighbor."

" What a comfort that will be ! " said Elizabeth. " It was only a little while ago that we were saying we wished we had a neighbor, and I was telling how much I missed Mrs. Ayres."

"It is a custom," continued the Captain, "when a new settler comes in, for the old residents who are all settled to give him a lift about putting up his house. I thought I would ask you to aid Watson, with the rest of us, when he comes."

"Certainly I will," replied Hugh; "but if I were going to begin, I would not build my house till I had made my burn. A man going into the woods in a hurry claps his house up anywhere, and hardly ever gets it where he wants it. Besides, he is in great danger of burning himself up in first clearing his land, when he has no open spot on which to set his house. Watson can come here and live with us in welcome, this summer. He will be convenient to his work; we've room to spare, enough to eat, and a plenty of milk for the children. Then, after he has been about on his place three or four months, has become acquainted with it, and knows what he wants, and where he wants his house, we will all turn out and put it up in a jiffy. Perhaps, too, he may leave on account of the war, and then he won't need any house."

"No, he won't," replied the Captain; "he is not one of that sort. But you are very kind indeed, and I think your advice is good. I will tell him of it, and also of your kind invitation. If he should accept it, we should take his wife and the children at our house."

"Tell him also," said Hugh, "that I have a heavy team, and when he makes his burn, will help him roll and pile his logs."

"Tell his wife," added Elizabeth, "that I join
heartily with my husband in the invitation."

The evening being now far spent, they parted
with mutual good wishes, and the Captain, mounting his horse, with his wife behind on a pillion, was
soon lost in the shades of the forest.

Hugh and Elizabeth that night builded many
castles in the air as they sat by the fire. " Now that
we have wool and flax," she said, " I mean that you
and the children shall have something better to wear
than leather breeches ; for although they are strong
and warm when it is dry weather, they are not very
comfortable when it is wet."

This season Hugh proposed to build a framed barn,
and also to board and shingle the roof of the house,
and to build a brick chimney. He and William
reckoned they could make the bricks, and they knew
they could make the shingles. But all these pleasant anticipations were to be dashed, and the McLellans were to be called to greater trials than they had
ever yet experienced. Still, as though to strengthen
them for it, Providence was allotting them a year
of unalloyed happiness.

The last of another May was now come, the planting was finished, and Hugh had determined, before
the hoeing came on, to cut his barn-frame. Settlers
were joining them now also. John Reed made his
clearing between them and Captain Phinney, just
over the brook. Then came William Bryant, and
made his between Reed and Phinney.

" Look here, husband," said Elizabeth, one evening; " here is Bryant with a family, and Reed, and Watson, and others are coming : I don't see what there is to hinder our having a school for all the children in the neighborhood. We might take one of the front rooms, and put in some benches, and fix it for a school-room, in the summer at any rate ; and if you build your brick chimney, we might then make fireplaces in the other rooms as well as in the kitchen, and so we could use it in the winter. What a great thing it would be for the children ! Here they are all the time with the Indian children, and they will grow up just like them ; and yet it is but little time that you or I can get to instruct them."

" But where shall we get a schoolmaster ? " inquired Hugh.

" Why, there is Sarah Phinney, she has good learning. You can all club together and hire her."

" Whether I build the chimney or not," said Hugh, " I will put a stone fireplace in there just like this in the kitchen, and I will go and see if the rest will join me ; and if not, we will hire her ourselves. It is just as much our duty to give our children learning as it is to give them bread. I think the neighbors will like it in the summer; but in the winter how could the children get here ? "

" The older ones could come on snow-shoes, and haul the younger ones on a sled. They might be obliged to lose a good many days, but it would be a great deal better than nothing."

Hugh found the others of the same mind, and he accordingly put in some benches, and secured the teacher; and the next week the school was under way. William could not be spared all the time, as Hugh needed his help in hoeing and haying; but he went three days in the week, and in haying-time Elizabeth went out and worked, she was so anxious that her son should go to school. Abigail was also taken from school in haying-time to help do the housework, that her mother might work out-doors, and let William be in school; for in those days it was thought more necessary that boys should have instruction than girls. William, as you very well know, was extremely fond of hunting, and also of shooting with the bow (for he did not abandon that even after he had his gun), and going to school almost deprived him of this sport, because on Saturdays, when there was no school, he was most of the time obliged to help his father. Yet William was glad of the privilege of going to school, because he was a wise and good boy, and saw the importance of it, and also saw how earnest his parents were for it. Besides, William did not roam in the woods shooting merely to please himself, but to procure something to live upon; and he could not have gone to a school before, even if there had been one, because he would have had to hunt to support the family. Indeed, all seemed delighted with the school, except Bose, who couldn't appreciate the advantages of learning. He was cross and uneasy enough, because he wanted William to go hunting with him; and so he would go to the door of the school-room, and whine and scratch till William would come out to still him, and then he would go and jump up to the hooks where the gun was kept, and bark, and then run to William, and put his fore-paws on his shoulders, and lick his face, and look *so* wishful, and say as plain as a dog could say, "Now, William, I do want you to take that gun and go into the woods with me; do, William!"

Mr. Watson soon began to fell trees and prepare for his burn. Leaving his wife and children at Captain Phinney's, he came to live with the McLellans. On Saturday nights he went home to his family, and sometimes also in the week. His wife would frequently take her knitting or sewing, and come down to take tea, bringing perhaps Mrs. Phinney and the children. They and Elizabeth's children would play together, and, if they could get a chance, would all steal off to the brook to frolic with the Indian children. Mrs. Watson would often stop all night, and then Elizabeth had somebody to talk with and consult about her work. Sometimes she would bring down wools, and sit and card while Elizabeth wove; and sometimes she would bring flax, and get Elizabeth to spin it, while she would get into the loom and weave, or would cut and make some dress for the children, for she was very capable in such things; but she could not spin flax and make it look as nice as Elizabeth could. Thus they aided each other, and were like sisters.   As they sat together thus in the afternoons, they chatted over their work, and had the best times imaginable.   Elizabeth was keen of wit and possessed great descriptive powers, and she would tell of odd things that had occurred in Ireland, so that Mrs. Watson would laugh till she cried.   No one would have thought, to hear them, that a terrible war was impending, that massacre was almost at their very doors, and that they knew it.   Mrs. Watson had great skill also in coloring with bean-leaves, and willow-bark, and sumach, and all kinds of roots. One day Elizabeth brought a piece of bright-red cloth, and, laying it in her lap, said, "What do you think of that?"

   "O, what a clear, beautiful red!" she exclaimed.
   "Handsome, is it not?"
   "Never saw anything like it.   Will it wash?"
   "Yes, it is a real fast color.   What do you suppose I colored it with?"
   "Dye-wood that you got at Saco, or cochineal."
   "No; I colored it with the leaves and blossoms of a plant that old Molly, the Indian whom you saw here the other day, gave me."
   "Why didn't you ask her what it was?"
   "I did, but she wouldn't tell.   I don't suppose she would have given it to me, only she was hungering for some tobacco, and she heard me tell William that he would have to take the horse and go to Saco, or somewhere, and get me some red dye.   Then she said that, if I would give her the tobacco, she

would get me some red dye that would never fade as long as the grass grew ; and I believe she has been as good as her word. I am astonished when I see what gifts the Almighty has given to these poor savages. Why, they can color their skin robes, and belts of wampum, and the things they keep for great occasions ; and porcupine-quills they can color red, or blue, or yellow, and they will last better than ours, with all our knowledge."

" Did you put alum in it ? "

" Yes, she told me to ; but they don't ; they put into it the juice of some other herb that has the same effect. They won't tell these things, although sometimes they will color things for me ; but it is just as they happen to feel : at other times you could not hire them to do it. It is my opinion that only a few of them know these things, and they keep the secret just as our dyers do, and that old Molly is one of these, because she is always at work upon such things, and does not do so much of the drudgery as the other Indian women. I hardly ever see her bringing wood."

It was equally pleasant for Hugh, after working and living so many years alone, to have Watson to talk with when he came in from his labor ; and the two men contrived to get together, as well as their wives, without hindering their work ; and so they became as fast friends as their wives. When Watson first came, Hugh said to him, " Now, Mr. Watson, we are to be very near neighbors, and as all men are

liable to err, I want you, if ever you have any matter against me, to tell me of it before you do anybody else, and I will do the same on my part." And
this wise and Christian habit kept them close friends
till death. They were very useful to each other,
too. Watson, though an excellent farmer and a
very intelligent man, having had far greater advantages than Hugh, had no mechanical gift, and could
scarcely make a sled-stake; but Hugh could do anything with wood, and could even shoe an ox or horse
in case of necessity. Watson took Hugh's advice
about building, and found it wise, for he finally set
his house in the middle of the very piece he had
preferred to burn over.

"How lively it seems now!" said Hugh. "Ever
since I was a boy I worked in a ship-yard with large
gangs of men, and even after I came to the colonies.
But since I came to this place, I have worked month
after month alone in the forest, where I could hear
nothing but the echo of my own axe, the chattering
of a squirrel, or the sound of wind among the trees.
Now I can hear the sound of your axe in one ear,
and that of Reed's in the other; and when the wind
is north-west I can hear Bryant's children as plain
as day, screaming and laughing, and Bryant driving
his oxen to plough."

But fearful rumors were now abroad; it was said
that war was inevitable between the mother country
and France; it was certain that the Indians would
be stirred up by France, and let loose upon the fron-

tier settlements; and Maine was all frontier, — Gorham (Narragansett) lying directly in the Indian trail.

In the latter part of May this state of suspense was turned into fearful certainty. An Indian runner in the service of the government brought word to Captain Phinney that England had declared war against France. All was now activity along the seacoast, arming forts, and building garrisons, and preparing for an attack from the French by water. But the danger of the settlers in Gorham was from the Indians. It was nineteen years since the last Indian war; but there were many whose parents, children, and friends had then fallen beneath the tomahawk. Many of the settlers had themselves fought, and its horrors were fresh in their recollection. But the excitement was somewhat allayed by the news that the government had made a treaty with all the Indians this side of the Penobscot River, and with the Penobscots, to take part on neither side; and so said the Indians themselves, who appeared as friendly as ever. Soothed by this report, the inhabitants, loath to leave their fields and lose their crops in order to build a garrison, continued at their labors as usual, in spite of the efforts of Captain Phinney, who put no trust in Indians or Indian treaties.

Hugh determined, instead of going into the woods to cut a barn-frame, as he had intended, to put his own house in a state of defence, rather than await the tardy movements of the rest. He first took off

10

the bark roof, and then, with some heavy timber, made a projection all round, and loopholed it, that he might be able to fire down upon any one coming to break the door or set the house on fire.   He put on a new roof and shingled it, first covering it with plank.   He then dug a small cellar under the floor, and stopped up the windows to the size of loopholes. Next he made a large trough, and put it within the house and filled it with water.   Finally he bought an additional gun, lead, powder, and flints, and, having made thorough preparations, went about his work as usual.   " If we were in garrison," said Hugh, " we should have to come out to work our lands ; and this house is now about as good as a garrison."

In the autumn Captain Phinney, Hugh, and the other near neighbors, all turned out and helped Watson put up his house, and a hovel or log barn for his cattle.   As they were all strong men and skilful at the business, having had abundant experience, the work went rapidly on ; and they made the house in rather a different manner from that in which we proceed in modern days, — *they built the chimney before they built the house.*   A fireplace in those days was an enormous thing ; it was like a great cave ; you might stand under the mantel bar, and when it opened its mouth, it swallowed half a cord of wood.   The chimney in which this great fireplace was built was thirteen feet square, sometimes more ; the foundation was laid with great rocks, of which the jambs of the fireplace were also made. Daniel Mosier said that the easiest and quickest way was to build the chimney first, and then they could take the oxen and haul the rocks just where they wanted them, as there was no cellar, and put them right on to the work, instead of having to get them in at the door. So they made him master-workman of the chimney, — and a noble one he built, too ; and by the time he had the chimney up, the others had the logs cut and hewed, ready for the walls of the house, which they soon rolled and piled up. Captain Phinney gave Watson a cow and a pig ; Hugh gave him half a dozen hens and a turkey ; Elizabeth presented a beautiful linen tablespread, and cooked a dinner and carried it over, (she and Hugh helped to eat it ;) Mr. Bryant sent half a sheep, and Daniel Mosier a bushel of wheat-flour and a leg of bacon, — so that the family could begin life splendidly in their new home.

The government not being able to persuade the Saint John and Cape Sable Indians to remain neutral, declared war against them, and required the Penobscots to aid in subduing them. When Captain Phinney heard of this he said : " Now we shall have it before long. Dog won't eat dog ; you can't make the Indians fight against Indians, — at any rate such a tribe as the Penobscots ; with some of the remnants of broken-down tribes, like these Saco Indians, it might be done. They won't do it, and when the government insists on it, they will join the Canada

Indians and these around here and in New Hampshire against us."

Still the spring passed quietly, and the Indians
came as usual, and were apparently as friendly as
ever, although there was open war between the
government and the eastern Indians, and it was
said that the Penobscots had been seen with their
war parties.

During the summer Mrs. Phinney would frequently go over on a Saturday to take supper with her
daughter, calling at Hugh's either going or coming,
and often the Watsons and McLellans would " go a
piece " with her on her way home. So, on a Saturday night in July, 1745, Mrs. Phinney came down
after dinner with her husband to make her usual
call. As they came along on their way home by
McLellan's, he and Elizabeth were sitting in the
door, with Sarah, who had been keeping school,
and who was waiting for her father and mother.
" Come ! " said the Captain, " put on your things
and go along a piece with us."

Hugh complied, and the neighborly party proceeded till they came to the brook, when a curious
and comical scene met their view. On the northern
side of the brook were four Indian wigwams covered with bass-bark, and from the limb of a large
tree was hanging the carcass of a deer, from which
a squaw was cutting steaks and roasting them on
sticks stuck in the ground. Two other squaws were
making moccasins, while three men were at work

A Curious and Comical Scene. Page 149.

upon a birch canoe. But in the brook below were a whole bevy of Indian children, from ten to fourteen years old, with nothing on but their breech-clouts, mingled with whom were the white children, all apparently at the very summit of earthly enjoyment. They had built a dam across the brook, and in the pond formed by the flowing back of the water they had made three beaver lodges or houses, constructed in exact imitation of those made by the beavers themselves.

" The young rogues must have had older hands to help them make these houses," said Captain Phinney, " for they are true to the life."

There was a hole in the dam, and some of them were repairing it ; others were swimming with sticks of willow and alder for winter provision in their teeth, and sinking them before the doors of the houses with stones ; some were crawling on their knees in the water, with mud held in both hands up against their throats, which they carried to stop the break in the dam. All were imitating beavers ; and as their tawny backs glistened in the sun, they were not unlike those animals in appearance. Abigail McLellan was cutting willows with a hatchet, and Bryant's children and some Indians were crawling on their hands and knees and dragging them in their mouths to the water. "I wonder they don't try to gnaw the trees down," said Hugh ; " they do everything else."

While they were all thus busily at work, one bea-

ver walked on the dam and did not put his hand to
anything, but seemed a sort of sentinel, for every
little while he would slap on the water with his foot
for a tail, and then in an instant all the young savages would dive into the water and disappear, the
sentinel after them, and go into the houses that had
entrances under water, while the white children
would hide in the woods, and for a few moments all
would be as still as death; then the sentinel would
poke up his head and listen, and then utter a low
cry, upon which they would all come out and go to
work again. But the most singular actors in the
scene were the young Indians who were in the
banks of the brook. Beavers always make holes in
the banks, the entrances to which are under water,
but afterwards slanting upwards as they go in, so
that they are warm and dry. To these they flee
when their houses are disturbed. The urchins had
made holes in the banks, and every little while out
would come an Indian child; and as his head rose
above water, his black wet hair and skin shining, and
his eyes glistening like balls of fire with the excitement, the sight was so irresistibly ludicrous, that
the whole company burst into peals of laughter,
while the savages on the bank never moved a muscle, but kept on with their work as though uncon-
scious of the presence of visitors.

"O mother," cried Abigail, who now for the first
time caught sight of the party, "see, we are play-
ing beaver!"

"Only see there," said Elizabeth, pointing to the woods; "if there is not our William, as good an Indian as any of them!"

Sure enough, William was now seen in company with a young Indian, both armed with bows and arrows, with tomahawks in their belts, creeping on their bellies in the direction of the dam. When within a short distance, William, fitting an arrow to the string, drew the bow, and the shaft struck the sentinel on the back, who fell at once, but, though wounded, made out to roll himself into the water with a loud splash, alarming all the rest, who disappeared in an instant to the different retreats. All was now still, and not a beaver to be seen or heard. William and his companion, a fine-looking fellow, stood talking together in a low tone after the animals had disappeared.

"As I live," said Captain Phinney, who was listening, "they are talking Indian."

"Very likely," said Elizabeth. "William can talk Indian and give the war-whoop with the best of them. One reason why I was so anxious to have a school was to wean him and Abigail from them; but who can wonder that they are bewitched to get with them? I am sure this is worth going a mile to look at, and what capital fun it must be for them! Indeed, I almost wanted to go in with them. But see there — what are they going to do next?"

The two boys now approached the dam and cut a hole in it with their tomahawks, when the water began to pour out in a great stream, leaving the houses and the holes in the banks dry. The animals, now leaving their houses and holes, began to run for the woods on their hands and knees, imitating the slow gait of the beaver, which cannot run much faster than a frog can hop, although very active in the water. William and the Indian now attacked them, tomahawk in hand, chasing and knocking them on the head till they had dispatched them all. They then threw the bodies together in a great heap, and, giving the yell of victory, went away, probably to get help to carry off the game ; but no sooner were their backs turned, than all the dead beavers got up and ran away.

"Do you suppose," said Hugh to Captain Phinney, "that these Indians, who have been here so many summers, and whom we have treated so kindly, will turn against us with the rest?"

"Do I? Yes, indeed! And as they know all about us, where the farms lie, and just how many of us there are, they will be just the ones to guide the French and other Indians to cut our throats. I wish I knew what those surly fellows are thinking about that are at work on that canoe. They have been here now four summers, and I have never seen a canoe amongst them ; now they are building one, and a large one too. It looks as though they expected to travel a great deal ; but you never can tell anything by an Indian's looks, as you can by a white man's. When they want to keep anything secret, there is no more expression in their faces than in an anvil. Neither can you torture or frighten them into telling anything. The whole Spanish Inquisition could not force a secret from an Indian's lips. I sometimes have a great mind to get the neighbors together and take them all prisoners, before they have time to get away and become spies and enemies. There would be so many guns and tomahawks the less to dread. All that prevents me is, that it would hasten matters, and bring the Indians that are camped around Sebago Pond upon us before we are ready. My son Edmund has been up there hunting, and he says there are twenty there, that there are very few squaws and children with them, that some of them had new guns of French make, and that their knives were new. If we only had the garrison built, I would do it in a moment, so sure do I feel that they are meditating mischief.

" There is scarcely anything that an Indian will not do for liquor ; they never refuse it ; they will in winter sell the beaver-skins they need for clothing to get it. Highly as they prize a gun, I have known them, when they had been drinking a day or so, to barter one for rum. Liquor will also do what nothing else will, — unlock an Indian's tongue, so that it will run like a mill-clapper. Often when in liquor they will let out what no threats, bribery, or coaxing could get from them sober. I offered old Molly's husband a pint of rum the other day, if he would drink it at my house, and stay the forenoon and fill the bottoms of some snow-shoes for me ; and, don't you think, the creature refused it! He offered to take the rum and the snow-shoes to his wigwam and do the work there ; but I wanted to set his tongue loose to find out what was going on. Still he refused, though he loves rum to distraction. I felt sure then that he suspected my design, and that there was something on foot which he was fearful he might, under the influence of liquor, let out to me."

"I should think," replied Hugh, "that William, understanding their lingo, would hear something dropped by the women or children."

"No," said the Captain, "they are not like us in that. Neither women nor children know the warriors' secrets ; besides, Indian women are as close-mouthed as their husbands."

"Do you suppose," inquired Elizabeth, "that old Molly would stand by and see William killed?"

"Yes, unless they could take him prisoner, and make an Indian of him, which wouldn't be a great task."

"Do you believe," said Elizabeth, "that the Beaver, as William calls that young Indian, who is his sworn friend, who has been his playmate this four years, who spends weeks sleeping in the woods by the same fire with him, would kill the Leaping Panther, as he calls William?"

"I suppose," replied Captain Phinney, "that the Beaver would now risk his life for William, and share the last morsel with him ; but if the Beaver had struck the war-post, and was painted for the war-path, and his Indian nature was up, he would glory in hanging William's scalp at his girdle."

" I cannot think so," said Elizabeth, glancing at the two boys, who, having finished their sport, sat by old Molly's fire, eating the deer-steaks she had been roasting for them.

In August, the government, finding the Penobscots were not only determined not to aid in subduing the other Indians, but were also, if they could not remain neutral, disposed rather to join with them, declared war against them, and offered a bounty equal to a hundred dollars in silver for each Indian scalp. But before the news had reached Gorham, William, going down one evening, as usual, to the Indian wigwams, found them deserted, and not an Indian to be seen. The settlers, now completely aroused and sure of immediate danger, set instantly to work upon the garrison, in order that they might put their harvest into it as it was gathered, and might keep the women and children in security.

The government had raised a company of rangers, who, guided by three friendly Saco Indians, scoured the woods. These reported that the Indians who had all summer been encamped at Sebago had disappeared. There was no longer any doubt that the savages had gone to Canada to receive instructions and arms, and would soon reappear as merciless and subtle foes.   William was greatly disturbed at the loss of his playmates, especially of the Beaver, with whom he had spent so many happy days.   He walked sadly over the silent spot lately so full of life ; he contemplated the desolate wigwams, whose bare poles were still standing, the blackened brands of the camp-fires around which he had eaten so many meals and listened to the tales of the older Indians, the marks at which they had been accustomed to shoot, and the remains of the old beaver-dam where they had enjoyed such glorious fun so recently.   But when he came to the place where they used to swim, and saw the rafts made of logs bound together with withes (one of which was then moored to the bank just as they last had left it), and the little birch canoes that the squaws made for them, and saw the footprints of his old playmates yet fresh in the clay, the tears came into the lonely boy's eyes in despite of himself, and he hasted, almost ran, from the spot.

CHAPTER VII.

PARTING OF BEAVER AND LEAPING PANTHER.

THE settlers, having now got in their hay and grain harvest, — and alarmed by the report that Indians had been seen in the town, and that they had killed a man and a boy at Topsham, and still more frightened by the news which Hugh received from his brother at Saco, " that the Indians had broken out, killed a man and forty head of cattle, and burned a garrison and saw-mill," — labored night and day to complete the defences of their garrison. It was erected on the highest land in the town, still called Fort Hill, close to the old burying-yard. The site of the present village of Gorham was then an unbroken forest, with the exception of a path through the woods to Portland, that could be traversed only on foot or horseback in summer, and with ox-teams in the winter. The garrison proper, which was already finished, was built of hewn timber twelve inches square; it was sixty feet long and fifty wide, being two stories high, the upper projecting three feet over the lower. In this projection, loopholes were made, through which the inmates could fire down upon any one attempting to set fire to the walls or burst open the door. At each corner were built flankers, projecting four feet beyond the walls on each side, and consequently sixteen feet square. In two of these, and at opposite corners, were two iron six-pounders, which raked the walls. These cannon, although owned by private persons, were taken to Portland for its defence at the time of the Revolution, and never returned. The roof was nearly flat, with merely sufficient pitch to shed water, built of timber and made tight by calking, which was done by Hugh, who, as we have seen, was bred to the business. All around the edge of the roof was a bulkhead of timber, bullet-proof and loopholed.

These loopholes were not much larger, on the outside, than the muzzle of a gun, but enlarged upon the inside, so as to range about ninety degrees. There was no well inside the walls, but the large roof was provided with spouts dug out of sapling pines, and the rain-water was caught in troughs. In the middle of the house was a great fireplace, where the inmates cooked their food in common. A portion of the lower story was reserved for the storage of provisions; the rest, with the entire upper story, was parted off into rooms, — some with partitions of hemlock bark, others with rough boards from Colonel Gorham's mill, at that time just finished, but afterwards destroyed by the Indians, — while some occupants made blankets and the skins of bears and deer serve their turn.

Every nerve was now strained to complete the additional defences, which consisted of a stockade, made of sticks of timber thirteen feet in length and ten inches thick, lined on the inside with hewn timber six inches thick. At the corners of the stock. ade, also, were flankers, which, after having been carried up thirteen feet, were floored over, and a watch-box built upon the top, which afforded an excellent lookout. The flankers, the walls of the stockade, and also the watch-boxes, were loopholed for musketry.

As the Indians were destitute of artillery, it is evident that a block-house built with so much care, and defended by men as resolute as the first settlers of Gorham, — many of them soldiers, and com manded by Captain Phinney, an old Indian fighter, — could never be taken by storm by any force they were able to bring. But the Indians were fertile in stratagems, and often succeeded in setting block-houses and stockades on fire by fastening pieces of lighted birch-bark to arrows, and shooting them into the roofs and walls. It was to guard against this, the greatest danger, that the roof was made flat, with a bulkhead around it, that they might keep it wet with the water from the troughs, which was not allowed to be used except in case of siege ; the water for daily use being brought from a spring on Captain Phinney's land, about fifty rods from the garrison, which has now been dry for many years by reason of the clearing of the land. The settlers cut away the forest for the space of three gunshots around this little pond, that the Indians might not be able to attack them from a covert in case they were reduced to the necessity of making a sally for water.

To the casual reader it might still seem that all the Indians had need to do, in order to compel a surrender, would be to sit down before the walls till the inmates were starved out, since they had no well within the fort, and only a limited stock of provisions; but in this respect the peril was in reality very little. The Indians lived only by hunting, and could stay before a garrison but a few days, when they were obliged to go and hunt for their own support; while, in the event of a siege, the first discharge of cannon would be heard at Portland, Saco, Windham (then called New Marblehead), and Scarborough, where were garrisons and soldiers.

During the winter the Indians made no attacks, for fear of being tracked by the scouts. The settlers then lived upon their farms, removing to the garrison only in the spring, or when an attack was feared. It was not so much the numbers or the prowess of the Indians that gave birth to the agony of those long, terrible years, but their subtlety and untiring patience when bent on plunder or revenge.

While in the fort, the settlers were comparatively safe, and in the winter unmolested; but then, on the other hand, by reason of the previous summer's crop being cut off by Indian attacks, they were often left at the point of starvation.

With the opening of spring came the Indian, thirsting for blood, with eye that knew not pity, and arm ever raised to strike. The cattle, absolutely necessary for the white people's support and the cultivation of the soil, must go to the pastures and woods; and each night they must be driven to the garrison yard; while the savages, with eyes keener than the serpent's, lay in ambush to slay or capture those who sought them. Indeed, the Indians often left the cattle unmolested during a whole season, though pinched with hunger themselves, in order that they might prove decoys to bring the owners within swing of their tomahawks.

Not a load of firewood hauled to the garrison, not a pail of water brought from the springs, but had its attendant risk; every path of daily life and labor was beset; the prostrate windfall, the hollow log, the tufted tree-top, the rank grass and rushes of the gullies, and even the very beds of the brooks, concealed a pitiless foe. The cracking of a dry stick sent a thrill to the stoutest heart, and all summer long the air was full of tomahawks. That beautiful season of the year, the Indian summer, with its soft hazy atmosphere and rich hues of fading foliage, was fraught with no pleasant associations to the anxious settler, for it was the chosen period for the savage to make his final and most fearful attack. In addition to all this, after laboring with scanty nourishment through the day, they were compelled to stand guard at night, lest the

11

savages, mounting upon one another's shoulders, should scale the walls or thrust fire into the loopholes. In this latter duty the men were often aided by the women, who nobly bore their share of the heavy burden. Let the boys and girls who read this ponder well the hardships our fathers endured that their children might be better off than themselves.

"William," said Hugh, one morning, about the middle of September, "I want you to dig a potato-hole in the western field ; you will find four stakes there, that I have stuck up to mark it out. Dig it four feet deep. I'll give you two days to do it in. It is easy digging, and if you do it in less time, you may have the rest of it to yourself. I am going up to hang the gates of the stockade, which will take me two days, and then our fort will be finished."

The middle of the first afternoon soon came ; so eager was William to finish his stint, in order that he might have time to beat up the quarters of a wolf which Bose had discovered, that he had forgotten to take his gun with him. He had buried himself to his shoulders in the pit, and was working as for dear life, when, hearing a noise, he stood up on his shovel, and, looking over the heap of earth he had thrown out, saw that all the cattle were in the field and making for the corn. Having driven them out, he began to put up the fence which ran along the edge of the woods ; but scarcely had he put up the first log, when, happening to look up, he beheld an Indian in his war-paint within a few feet of him. It was evident to William, at the first glance, that his intentions were by no means hostile; his gun, though within reach of his hand, was placed against the butt of a pine, while its owner, with arms folded upon his chest, stood gravely regarding him.

William had never before seen a savage accoutred for war, and he resolutely gazed, and with admiration, upon the startling apparition. His legs were incased to the thigh in stockings of dressed deerskin, ornamented (as were also his moccasins) with porcupine-quills dyed with bright colors; on his loins he wore a covering of red cloth, the ends of which hung in a flap behind and before, and were fringed and covered with Indian bead-work; in this covering was a pocket containing parched corn, and a flint and steel, with tinder made of the fungus that grows on the birch. His head was shaved, except a space of three or four inches wide, extending from the crown to the nape of the neck, which was divided into portions plaited together, and made so stiff with bear's grease that it stood erect; the hair was pulled out of his eyebrows, and his forehead down to the eyes painted red; the rest of his body, which was naked, and his face, were painted with alternate stripes of red and black. The whole figure wore a frightful aspect, and, contemplated amid the gloom of the forest, was a thing to try the strongest nerves. In his belt were a tomahawk and an ammunition-pouch; and his scalping-knife was hung by a thong to his neck, while, to complete his equipment, a bow and quiver of arrows hung from his shoulder, secured by a band around the breast. The reason why the Indian encumbered himself with the bow, when in possession of the rifle, was, that the discharge of a gun would betray his whereabouts to the quick ears of his enemies, especially to the rangers employed by the government to scour the woods and follow the trail of the savages, who, being stimulated by a twofold motive — the desire of obtaining the bounty of a hundred and sixty-five dollars for Indian scalps, and the thirst for vengeance — were ever on the alert. With the bow and arrow he could without noise kill game for his sustenance, and they were likewise of great importance as saving powder and lead, for which the savage often had to travel hundreds of miles, and which were articles too precious to be lavishly expended.

William thought he had never beheld a grander sight than this warlike savage. But he could scarcely credit the testimony of his senses, when through the thick coat of paint he verily thought he perceived the features of his old playmate, — in short, that the stern, collected being before him was no other than the Indian lad whose laugh but a few months ago rang shrilly through the forest, and than whom none had been more light-hearted and frolicsome. In that brief period he seemed to have increased both in height and bulk, and, though but little older than William, to have leaped at once from a boy to the estate of a man. In a tone of mingled doubt and anxiety, William exclaimed, "Beaver, can this be you?"

The Indian extended his hand in silence, which William eagerly grasped. Drawing himself up with all the dignity of a chief who counted his scalps by scores, Beaver thus addressed his wondering playmate:

"Leaping Panther, listen! Two moons ago I was a boy and played with the boys; I helped the squaws to pound the corn, get the wood for the fire, carry the canoes, and bring to the wigwam the meat the hunters had killed. Now I am a warrior. I have struck the war-post of my tribe; I have listened to the aged men, into whose ears the Great Spirit has whispered in their dreams, when the moose has lain down to rest, and the souls of the dead come back to ask why their blood is not avenged. I have heard the great war-chiefs tell their deeds — how they struck the enemies of our tribe, bound them to the stake, and made them cry like squaws; and I have seen their scars of battle. When I too shall have taken many scalps, the maidens of my nation will contend to cook my food, light my pipe, and bring the meat to my lodge when I return from the hunt, to cover my moccasins and my leggings with ornaments, and pound my corn. Then I shall wear the eagle's feather, and be counted with the chiefs at the council-fire.

"When the Master of Life calls me, I shall go to the southwest, where are the happy hunting-grounds

of my fathers.   There is no snow, there are no cold
winds, but the leaves are always green, the flowers
never fade, there is much game, and there bad Indians never come.

" Once we were children together ; then we were
like brothers.   It is not so long ago that it should be
forgotten.   We slept by the same fire, played in the
same brook, drank from the same gourd, divided
what we took in hunting ; one blanket covered us
both.   Those were happy days ; they were too short
for our pleasures, and we were sorry to see the sun
go down."   As he uttered these words, his voice
became musical, and his tones assumed an indescrib-
able pathos, that melted into the very heart of his
auditor, and brought the tears to his eyes.   Pausing,
he plucked from a rotten stump beside him two small
hemlocks, whose roots, as they grew side by side,
were twisted one around the other ; holding them
up, he said : " My heart is now soft, though it is the
heart of a warrior.   It is soft, because I call to mind
that once we were like these plants.   We grew side
by side, and as our roots became bigger, they grew
closer together ; but now, like these, we must also
be separated."   Tearing them asunder, he flung
them in opposite directions.   " We must now seek
each other's lives.

" Leaping Panther, listen !   Your people have
taken away our hunting-grounds, and cut down the
trees so that we have no meat for our squaws and
our little ones.   The blood of our young men, shed

by you, and not yet avenged by us, cries in our ears
so that we cannot sleep. Therefore we have dug up
the hatchet. We shall not bury it again till we
make it red with the white man's blood. Had I
wished to kill you, without alarming your people,
I could have done it with the bow or the tomahawk.
If Wenemovet or Wiwurna, or any of our old playmates, had been here instead of myself, your scalp
would have now been hanging at his girdle, or
drying in the smoke of the wigwam. But as I
watched you, my heart grew soft. I said, 'I will
speak to my brother. I will look in his eyes. We
will tear our hearts asunder, and then we will seek
each other's blood.' Do not therefore be afraid, but
speak. The ears of the Beaver are open."

"I am not afraid of you, Beaver, though you are
older than I am, have gun, knife, and tomahawk, and
look so 'skeerful' in your paint, while I am bare-
handed. Mother Molly called me leaping Panther
because I was so quick; I could jump on you and
throttle you before you could draw a knife or cock
a gun at me. Notwithstanding all your big talk
about being a warrior, and striking the war-post,
you never have seen (and it's my opinion you never
will see) the day when I couldn't lay you on your
back at rough and tumble, or at close hugs, and let
you have both 'under-holds' into the bargain. In
respect to your shooting at me unawares, I freely
say that you might have done it, just as easy as a
cat can lick her paw, and in that I owe you my life.

But that is no more than I should have expected at your hands; it is your nature, Beaver; you are a brave, good, true-hearted boy, and it's only your Indian bringing-up that will ever make you anything else."

A smile of pleasure flitted athwart the grave features of the Indian at this downright avowal from one he loved with all the intensity of savage passion.

" But tell me, Beaver, did the cattle tear that fence down ? "

" No; I tore it down."

" That you might shoot me when I came to drive them out ? "

" No; but I was afraid of being seen by your people, and I took that way to draw you to my ambush."

" It was well planned, and you are rightly called Beaver, for the beaver is wise, and I doubt not you will be a great chief. But you have taught me a lesson. The next time I will let the cattle eat the corn before I will go to drive them out without a gun.

" Well," continued William, " if your heart grew soft when you saw me this morning, so did mine the day after you went away. You know we — you and I and Conuwass — were going to hunt porcupines in the hard woods on Watson's hill, and your mother was going to work me a belt just like yours. I got up early, and tied Bose up, — for the old fool will shake a porcupine, and get his nose full of quills, — caught my gun, and ran with all my might to your wigwam.   When I got there, you were all, all gone.   Then I went down to the brook.   There I found the rafts and the canoes, and all the things just as we had left them.   Then down to the swimming-place ; but when I saw your tracks there, O, it brought everything right up, and the place looked so lonesome I couldn't stay, but went back home.   I went into the barn to untie Bose, and when he saw the gun in my hand, he began to jump up on me, and lick my face, thinking he was going a-hunting. I said, ' Bose, you will never more have any such good times as we have had, because Beaver is gone, and we shall never see him again.'   I had made out to hold in till then, but the minute I spoke your name the tears would come.   I sat down and cried like a baby."

In the course of this conversation the boys had drawn nearer and nearer to each other, until at length they seated themselves side by side on a windfall, and somehow their hands got locked together.

" That was wrong, Panther ; only squaws do that."

" I don't see why a man shouldn't cry, as well as laugh, especially if he can't help it."

" He should do neither ; a warrior should never behave as a squaw ; he should be like a rock."

"I know what you mean," was the rejoinder.

" You think it makes against a man's courage to
have a tender heart; but it don't. Now, there's my
mother. If the sun should fall right out of the sky,
it wouldn't scare her. For all that I saw her cry
when she thought Mrs. Watson was going to die.
Father is tender too, but your whole tribe couldn't
frighten him, or make him cry, unless he had a mind
to. There is our Alec — Little Snapping Turtle.
When he gets crying mad, then look out for yourself; he'll let you have hot coals, hatchet, anything
that comes to hand; but nothing scares him."

" You can never be a warrior, Panther, while you
feel thus."

" I never want to be."

" Don't want to be? "

" No.   I had rather hoe corn, or hunt, than fight
just for the sake of fighting. I think it is just the
poorest business a man can follow, except it is his
duty."

" I see, Panther, the Great Spirit has given to the
white man a different heart from the Indian's. I
love to kill — every Indian does; I love to see blood
run; I should like to eat the flesh and drink the
blood of the enemies of my tribe."

While he spoke the savage gleamed from his
whole face ; his eyes glared, his nostrils dilated, and
his features, seen through the terrors of the war-
paint, were those of a fiend. The instincts of his
companion, nursed at the breast of a Christian
mother, and imbued with the principles of religion,

volted at this display of a wolfish nature. He coolly replied, " I wouldn't. I should rather drink buttermilk. If an Indian had injured me, I should want satisfaction from him ; it would not do me any good to kill some other Indian, who never had injured me, just because he was an Indian ; or to murder a little innocent babe in the cradle, because his father or grandfather had injured me or my grandfather before he was born."

" That is our custom," replied Beaver. " Our fathers and wise men have always done so, and taught us to do so, and therefore it is right."

" I don't care who taught it, or whose custom it is," replied his sturdy antagonist. " It ain't right nohow ; that stands to reason. It's clean against Scripture and the Catechism too. You say that after this we must seek each other's lives because our fathers have injured one another. I've heard my father and mother say, a hundred times, that they never lost so much as a hen, or a kernel of corn, by the Indians, and that, so far as that was concerned, they didn't want any better neighbors than the Indians, — that they should have starved to death one winter but for the Indians. I am sure no Indian will say that we ever wronged him, or took his land, for we bought our land and paid for it. No more did our ancestors hurt them, for they are all on the other side of the sea, and never saw an Indian."

" Do not think, Panther, that the Indians do

not know what is just. I have heard my people talk, and I know that, if you were living here alone, and no other white people here, no Indian would lift his tomahawk against you; and if you were hungry, they would share with you their provision, be it little or much. They know very well that you are not like the white men who were in the Narragansett war, who had their land given them because they killed the Indians; that you bought your land, although you bought it of those who killed the Indians; but that was not your fault. They know, too, that your speech is different from theirs, that your actions are different, and that there is no Indian blood on your hands, which are clean. But if you go with the rest to fight the Indians, you must expect they will kill you."

"I expect you to kill me if you can, in a fair stand-up fight, or an ambush, when our peoples ambush one another. But I don't see why we, that have been like brothers together, should pick each other out, and go skulking around, in the places where we used to play, to kill each other."

They remained a long time silent. At length the Beaver, rising, replied:

"Panther, I have thought of your words, and they are good. Not one of my tribe but would have slain you to-day. If the warriors knew that I had not done thus, they would blush with shame. When I set out on the war-path, I said, 'I will speak to the Panther; after that, he will be on his watch;

then my heart will be very hard. I know where he works, where he hunts, and where he plays. I will ambush him every step he takes. I will kill the dog, and then I shall the more easily kill him. I will hang his scalp at my girdle, and the warriors of my nation will rejoice. They will say that Beaver will be a great chief. He has slain the Panther, whose claws were almost grown, who could throw the tomahawk, and shoot the eye out of a squirrel, and who would have slain many of our people.'

" But your words have changed my heart, as the maple-leaves change beneath the fingers of the frost. We will not stain with each other's blood the places where we have hunted and fished and played together. Only when our tribes meet on the war-path will we be foes. When the Beaver thinks of the Panther, and of the long summer days they have hunted and played together, and sat by the same fire, it shall be like a pleasant dream of the night; there shall be no blood on it. Is it well? "

As the Beaver uttered these words, it was evident that it required all the stoicism of his Indian nature and training to keep down the tender emotions that were struggling to betray themselves. His face, despite the terrors of the war-paint, assumed a noble, touching expression, and his voice was feminine in its low music.

William was touched to the very heart, and being less able to control his feelings, his eyes filled with tears, and his voice trembled, as he replied, " It is well ! "

The Indian resumed his gun, and, extending his hand to William, they exchanged a parting grasp, and he was soon lost in the depths of the forest.

William remained listening to the light step of his playmate till it was no longer audible. Then, seating himself on the ground with his back to a tree, he ran over in his mind the happy days they had spent together, till he was at length aroused by the trampling of the cattle, which, having got a taste of the grass, were again going through the gap into the field. He saw with surprise that it was almost sundown, and that his mother, alarmed by his not returning to supper, was coming after him with a gun on her shoulder, accompanied by Bose. The dog, after jumping on William, put his nose to the ground, and instantly started on the track of the Indian; but William called him back. He then sat down on the ground, and began to growl and whine and run his nose into the dirt.

"William," said his mother, "look at that dog! There are Indians around! What made you come without your gun?"

"Yes, mother," replied William; "there is an Indian round here; but he won't injure us."

"But what is the matter with you, William? How came this fence down? You have been crying! I saw you sitting here with your face between your hands, the cattle going into the field right before your eyes, and I thought you must be wounded."

"I can't talk now, mother; don't ask me now.

When we get home I'll tell you all about it. Bose, drive the cows home!" But Bose, reluctant to leave the Indian's track, required a second command, coupled with a little kick, before he would obey.

Elizabeth, though tenderly attached to her children, ruled them with a stern, though kind hand, and exacted of them unquestioning obedience. But she was possessed of great discernment of character, and with William, who was peculiarly thoughtful and affectionate, and seldom manifested any desire to overstep the limits of duty, she abated somewhat of the stern authority she exercised over the other children, who were of more rugged natures, — especially Mary (our own grandmother), and Martha (Grannie Warren), to whom we are indebted for the facts of this story, and who both of them greatly resembled herself; and so also with Alexander, who was a very devil for grit, and, as his father said, would have made a good moss-trooper.

CHAPTER VIII.

THE INDIAN WAR.

A T the day of which we write, the intercourse between parents and children was much more formal than at present. The people were then living under a monarchy, and the spirit of the government was felt in the family. Deference to superiors in age or station was rigidly exacted In many families children did not eat with their parents, but at a side-table in the same room. School-children were required to " make their manners " to their teachers and to aged people or strangers whom they met in the road, going to or returning from school ; the boys took off their hats and made a bow, the girls made a courtesy, — that is, they bent the knees, and depressed the body, very much as ladies do now when a person treads on their dress in the street. And this was a good custom : it taught children politeness, and made them easy in their manners, and so civility became habitual, because it had grown in them. They did not stand in the middle of the road, thumb in mouth, staring at a stranger, but made their manners and passed on.

Parents were not accustomed to take their children in their laps and kiss and caress them, — not after they were babes. I should have been frightened if my father had kissed me when I was a child. But they loved them just as well as parents love their children at this day, for all that, and were willing to endure the greatest hardships, death itself, in order that their children might have greater advantages than they themselves had enjoyed. Thus it was with Elizabeth and Hugh: they were not accustomed to caress their children, and their parental word or look was law, and neither to be questioned nor disobeyed. "Mother says so," was reason enough.

His mother assisted William to put up the fence, after which they took their way in silence to the house. As they reached the door, Bose, having yarded the cows, was stealing around the corner of the pig-sty, and making for the woods. He could not get the Indian's track out of his head, and, as William would not go with him, was determined to go "on his own hook."

"Bose, you villain you!" cried William, "come here, sir!" He had never spoken so to Bose before. The dog came slowly towards him, his ears drooping, his tail between his legs, his belly dragging on the ground, and with an astonished, supplicating

12

look. William took him by the nape of the neck, and dragging him into the house, tied him to the bedstead, exclaiming, " You shall stay there at any rate till the scent is washed out ! "

He now shut the door, and fastened it to keep the other children out, and, sitting down before his mother, told her the whole story word by word. He told her what Beaver said, and how he answered him. " As long, mother, as he talked about his striking the war-post, and being a brave, and killing folks, and swelled up so, and seemed so big, and to think he was so much better than I was, I didn't care — I should just as lief have fought with him as not. But you can't tell how it made me feel when he came to talk so to me as he did at the last of it. I had half a mind to go off with him ; but something held me back. I suspect it was because I thought how he looked when he said he liked to see blood run, and that he could drink it."

" O William ! " cried his mother, now thoroughly alarmed and distressed, " could you leave me and your father and your brothers and sisters, and go to be an Indian, and live with savages ? " and, breaking through all the restraints and the customs of that day, she put her arms around his neck, and took his head upon her knees.

" No, mother," he replied at length, " I could never leave you. But I did love Beaver so ! You know I had nobody else to play with, as Uncle James's boys have at Saco, and we agreed so well;

and I've heard you yourself say, that, if he was an Indian, a better boy never stepped. When I saw how bad he felt (though he kept it down), and his voice sounded so, it did cut me deep. O mother, I don't know what to do with myself ! '' Then the great boy, fairly getting into his mother's lap, put his arms around her neck and sobbed like a little child.

It was the first sorrow and the first parting, and the "bitterness thereof drank up his spirit." Elizabeth, who had endured so many bitter trials herself, was deeply touched ; all the mother was aroused by the agony of her son. She pressed him to her bosom, ran her fingers through his hair, and kissed him as she had done when he was an infant. At length she persuaded him to lie down, and, sitting by him, soothed him, till, worn out by his feelings, he was sleeping for sorrow.

The piety of Hugh and Elizabeth was not something put upon them, narrow and bounded by the Sabbath and the family altar, but the offspring of their affections. They prayed not only at stated times, but whenever they were moved to do so. They "walked with God," and when they wished to say anything to Him, as to their father, they said it. If Hugh was building fence beside the woods on a pleasant spring morning, when the ground was steaming and the fences smoking in the warm sun, the robins singing and the wild geese *honking* overhead, — if the beauty of the scene, the promise of the year, or some blessing he had received, drew out his heart in gratitude to God, — the strong man, who, if he feared God, feared nothing else, would drop his axe, and retiring to the woods, pour out his soul in grateful prayer and praise.

Thus, when Elizabeth (after having spread the table for William when he should awake) sat down beside the bed, and thought over the circumstances he had related to her, considering the ripeness of judgment and sterling qualities both of mind and heart which he had manifested, and how fearlessly and nobly he had borne himself, she straightway knelt down and thanked her Maker for the boy, for his preservation from the bullet of the Indian, and that he had not been mastered by his feelings of attachment to his companion and his love for life in the woods, and gone off with the savage.

The history of those days proves abundantly that it is much easier to pass from civilized to savage life, than it is to emerge from the state of the savage to that of civilized man. And taking into consideration the boy's attachment to his friend, and his passionate love for the free life of the woods, his mother had the best of reasons for anxiety. During that same year, a lad by the name of Samuel Allen was taken by the Indians at Deerfield. Though he had been with them but eighteen months, "yet, when his uncle went to redeem him, he refused to talk English, would not speak to his uncle, and pretended not to know him, and finally refused to go home, and had to be brought off by force. In his old age he always declared that the Indian's life was the happiest."

William, after an hour's sleep, rose calm and refreshed. No slight cause could long disturb his well-balanced and healthy nature, and his emotions soon became subject again to his control. His mother placed food before him of which she knew he was fond, and, sitting down to the table with him, exerted herself to turn the conversation into a cheerful channel. While they were eating, Hugh came in and joined them at their meal.

When the children were put to bed, the three drew their stools around the fire, and entered into an anxious consultation in respect to their duty under the circumstances. It was probable that Beaver was only one of a body of savages on the war-path, who had committed the violence at Saco and Topsham and Purpooduck, and were watching for an opportunity to strike another blow. Ought they not instantly to give the alarm, in order that the settlers might be on their guard, and that they might, with the help of Bose, follow on the track of Beaver, and thus prevent the meditated blow, or capture him? Ought any feelings of good-will to him to influence them so far as to put in peril the lives of their neighbors? Perhaps before another morning they might hear the sound of the war-whoop.

It was their duty perhaps, at that very moment,

to alarm the nearest neighbors; under cover of night
to get as silently as possible to the garrison, and
fire the alarm-gun, thus putting Mosier and the
more distant inhabitants on their guard.

Thus reasoned Hugh and Elizabeth. On the
other hand, William earnestly, though respectfully,
opposed. He said that it was as clear as day to
him that Beaver was neither a spy nor one of a
party lying in ambush; for the Indians would never
send so young a person on so dangerous and important an errand; that Beaver wouldn't have dared
to spare him if he had been a spy, when he could
have taken his life without noise, because they
would have asked him where he had been, and
what he had done; and that Beaver had told him
that his own people would never know where he
had been.

"Why, father," said William, "I had my back to
him, putting up the fence; I turned round to look
for a pole, and there he was, standing right behind
me, and must have been standing there as much
as fifteen minutes. He could have driven his tomahawk through my skull, or knocked me on the
head with the breech of his gun, or shot me right
through the back with an arrow, and I never
should have known what hurt me. I believe that
he came back on purpose to bid me good-by, as he
didn't have time when they went away. I know
Beaver wouldn't lie — he would think it mean for a
warrior to lie, — and he said that was what he came

for. I know that he had come a great way, and come fast too, for his moccasins and leggings were scratched and torn, he was spattered with clay, and the sweat had made the stripes of paint on his breast all mix together and run down on to his belt, and streak it all over, and he seemed beat out. There was but a little corn in his pouch; it wasn't half full. He had a new French carbine. and his tomahawk and knife were new, and he had a breech-clout of broadcloth. I believe that they all went right from here to Canada to get their outfit, and that the rest of them are there to-night."

Although Hugh was well aware that William's judgment was far beyond his years, that a kind of instinct in respect to all matters of forest life, and a thorough knowledge of Indian habits, gave to his opinions a weight to which neither his age nor experience entitled them, yet he was astonished at the keen observation with which the lad had noted every part of the Indian's equipment, and the maturity of mind evinced by the conclusions drawn from it.

" How mean it would be, mother, when he has just spared my life," said William, in conclusion, " and we have agreed not to pick each other out, to go and set Bose and the Rangers on his trail ! I'd rather be shot, any day."

" Well, William," replied his mother, " it is just as your father says. He knows what is best to be done."

After long deliberation, the father said, " Wife, I think the boy is right. This Indian was so much attached to him, that the thoughts of his old playmate haunted him night and day, and he could not rest till he had seen him again. And I shouldn't wonder if he had travelled all the way from Canada to do it. A hundred or even five hundred miles is not much to an Indian. When they have an object ahead, they will tire out any animal but a wolf. — William, look to the priming of the guns, and let us go to bed. It does not become Christian people to be outdone in generosity by a savage."

The next day the defences of the garrison were completed, and everything made ready for the inhabitants to move in. The guns were mounted in the flankers, a common stock of ammunition provided, and a flag-staff erected, upon which was hoisted his Britannic Majesty's flag. The Indians, discouraged, perhaps, by the evident preparation to give them a warm reception, notwithstanding their recent outbreak, left the Gorham settlers unmolested. It was evident that the Indians had no desire for a conflict; that they were well aware that it was more for their interest to trade with the English than to fight with them, since, though they might obtain successes at first, they were sure to get many hard knocks, and to be defeated in the end; that it was only by reason of French influence they engaged in the war at all; but those best acquainted with them believed that, after the first outbreak, they had gone back to Canada, to return in the spring with greater numbers, and thoroughly armed and prepared for conflict.

In view of this probable event, nine of the eighteen families of which the clearing then consisted left their farms and removed, some to Portland, others to Massachusetts. Nine — those of Captain Phinney, Hamblen, Mosier, McLellan, Harvey, Reed, Cloutman, Hodgdon, and Eliphalet Watson — remained to face the storm, and perish, if need be, defending their firesides. The amount of peril which, according to the common opinion of that day, they incurred, may be estimated from a remark made in a letter written from Falmouth, in 1747, to the Hon. William Pepperell : * " I am now to inform you that ye barbarous and cruel sons of violence, on ye 14th inst., killed and scalped Na' Dresser, a young man, within thirty yards of David Libby's house. A scout of what few soldiers were here, with some of our inhabitants, immediately followed, came athwart of three camps, about half a mile above Gorham Town Garrison, where they found some beef and the skins of two cows. We are in poor circumstances, having but about 15 or 20 sol· diers to scout from Capt. Bean's to N. Yarmouth, so that the people cannot pretend, without the utmost hazard, to plant, or sow, or carry on any other business, especially on ye most out and exposed

* See Maine Historical Society's Collections, Vol. III.

parts. And unless immediate succor or assistance,
I cannot perceive how Gorham Town, Marblehead
(Windham), and Sacarappy can subsist, — for they
do not care to visit them, or carry them necessaries of life, unless they have more men."

Hugh, having an abundant harvest and a strong
team, spent the winter in lumbering, with greater
profit than ever before; but as the spring of 1746
approached, it was evident that the blow would not
be longer delayed. Captain Phinney, uneasy and
anxious by reason of the great forwardness of the
spring, — as the spring was the customary period
for the Indians to make their attack, — begged and
prayed the settlers to come to the garrison. All
except four families complied, — McLellan's, Reed's,
Bryant's, and Cloutman's. They determined to stay
out till they could get their ploughing and sowing
done.

We now crave the indulgence of our young readers while (for the sake of the Gorham boys and
girls) we give a passing glance at the condition of
the four families referred to, in order that they may
know more clearly how much their ancestors under-
went that their children might be better off than
they themselves.

Imagine yourselves in the flat ground to the east
of the Female Seminary. The road (such as it is) —
full of stumps and cradle-knolls and bushes, among
which a horse can pick his way in the summer, and

over which the ox-teams can go in the winter when
they are all covered with snow — runs from Sacca-
rappa up over Fort Hill to the river. You are on
Hugh McLellan's land, all surrounded by woods.
On your right hand, as you face north, is an opening
in the woods where, Grannie said, her father cut a
mast so large that they turned a yoke of oxen on
the stump of it without their stepping off. As you
descend the Academy hill, covered with a heavy
growth of rock-maple and yellow birch, you come in
sight of Hugh's log-house, which is on the western
side of the road, close to where the brick house now
stands, but nearer to the road and the brook. Some
pomegranates and an old cellar mark the spot. As
you cross the brook upon a fallen pine that serves
for a bridge, and ascend the hill on the other side,
you come to Reed's house, on the west side of
the road, just north of the house now owned by
George Pendleton, Esq. A little above Reed's, on
the opposite side of the road, on what was the Colonel Nathaniel Frost farm, lived Cloutman. About
fifty rods farther, on the west side of the road, you
come to Bryant's. This house stood on the north side
of the road that now crosses the Fort Hill road and
runs over towards Cressey's and Clement's Corner,
in the corner of the fence. Still going north, you
cross a little thread of water, that was quite a stream
once, at the foot of Nathaniel Hamblen's hill; on the
bank of this brook Bryant was killed, while fleeing
to the garrison. The road which you are in, full

of stumps and knolls, is now Fort Hill road, but was then called King Street. As you pass on, you find it crossed by another at right angles, which was then called Queen Street, and, after going a few rods, lost itself in the woods. Upon the east side, in the corner made by these two roads, on the north side of Queen Street, stood the house of Captain Phinney, near where Moses Fogg's house now stands. A short distance north of this house, on the west side of the road, is the meeting-house, built of logs, and erected when there were not more than twelve or fourteen families in town. At the door of it is the horse-block, — a great stick of tim- ber, one end on the ground, the other raised a few feet, thus, , for children and short-legged people, who could take the horse to the highest part of it, which was nearly level with the beast's back. During the war, worship was held in the southeast flanker of the fort, which stood just above the meet- ing-house. The road runs due north to the river, and south to where the Portland road now crosses it, whence it ran into the woods and was lost. Gorham Corner was then up at Fort Hill, what is now so called being all forest.

You must also know that your ancestors were very loving and sociable in their dispositions, had all things common (you know what Grannie said in the first chapter, when she was provoked), and stood by each other till the death. Of course they had no public amusements, and when they could they used to assemble at each other's houses to have a social meal and a good time, and to hear the news, for they had no papers. As they were very industrious, and the labor of clearing their land and providing for their families was very great, the custom on such occasions was for the women to go with their knitting or sewing, and some time (if work was very pressing) with wool and cards, soon after dinner, while the men came at four o'clock, and they all had supper at five, — while, in consequence of the expected rest, they exerted themselves so much that they did a good day's work before they went.

Upon the 16th of April, Wednesday, the families out of the garrison were invited to Bryant's to supper. Shortly after dinner the women were all on the spot with their children. Elizabeth had her children, — Abigail, now eight years old, Mary, six, Alexander, four, and Carey in arms. Cloutman's wife had her little boy Timothy, of eight years; while Mrs. Bryant had a family of five, the eldest a boy of twelve, and the youngest a babe but a fortnight old.

Mrs. Bryant was a large-boned, strong, fearless woman, with a freckled face, masculine voice, and a blustering way; she was an inveterate scold, but she was also generous, hospitable, kind in sickness, and always ready to do a good turn for anybody. She was a capital cook and housewife, and the neighbors, who were used to her ways, all liked her. Many of her people had been killed by the Indians, and she hated them with all her soul. In this respect she was the very opposite of Elizabeth, who always gave to them when it was in her power, and often in her own necessity, and so was always on the best of terms with them. But Mrs. Bryant would not allow that there was a single good quality in them. When they asked for anything, she would call them Indian dogs. And once she threw hot water on one who came to grind his tomahawk on their grindstone.

Reed's wife was a young woman with two small children.

In the course of the afternoon they had a very animated discussion in respect to the Indians. Mrs. Bryant gave it as her opinion (in which she was supported by Mrs. Reed and Mrs. Cloutman) that they were no better than wolves, if indeed as good, and ought to be knocked on the head at every opportunity. She then related with great glee a most shameful butchery of Indian women and children by her husband's father and other white men in the Narragansett war; to the propriety of which her supporters gave their assent by saying, " It served them right."

" Now, Mrs. Bryant," said Elizabeth, " I can't think that a Christian woman, and one so kind-hearted as I know you to be, could bear to see a little innocent babe that never injured anybody flung into a blazing fire, and another into a bog, and trodden to death in the mud and snow, before the eyes of its mother, even if that mother was an Indian squaw."

"Yes, I could, and glory in it. Nobody spares a rattlesnake because it's little ; it's a rattlesnake if it's only half an inch long, and will sting when it gets big enough."

"I am astonished, Mrs. McLellan," said Cloutman's wife, "that you, who profess to be a religious person, and are the wife of an elder in the church, should take up for those who have dealings with Satan! Why, don't you know that their conjurors can make a green leaf out of a dry one, can take an old cast skin of a snake out of a bush and turn it into a live reptile, and make water freeze right in the middle of the summer?"

"I don't believe any such nonsense," said Elizabeth, "or that they are any nearer to the Devil than any other wicked men. We are not to make ourselves even with them, and be perhaps worse than they are. There are allowances to be made for creatures that have never had the Gospel nor any kind of instruction. I am sure they are not one whit worse than the wild Irish we have had to deal with, but a great deal better."

"If," said Mrs. Reed, "you had had your own blood relations taken and fastened by a long rope to a beech-tree, so that they could walk round it, and then a fire built around them, and when they were all blistered with the heat to have a hole cut in their side, and one of their inwards pulled out and

fastened to a limb of the tree, and they whipped
with briers and fire-brands, and made to travel
round the tree till they pulled their bowels out,
and dropped down dead, I reckon you'd feel as we
do, and want to serve them the same sauce when
you had a chance."

"Indeed, Mrs. Reed, I can't feel as you do, nor
do I desire to," said this apostle of humanity. "I
believe, if we had been brought up like them, we
should have been much like them. Indeed, I have
read in the old books that our ancestors were no
better before they had the Gospel. And as to
what you say about my being a religious person, if
religion is to make me treat my fellow-creatures
worse, I don't want it. I don't blame the Indians
for defending their property ; it's my opinion they
have had hard usage. We never make a treaty
with them but to break it ; we never agree with
them upon a line, but we are the first to step over
it ; we tread on them, and when they turn on us
we call them wolves. No, I don't feel like you.
And were I, on my way home to-night, to find an
Indian child forsaken in the woods, if I could not
preserve its life in any other way, I would nurse it
at my own breast before I would destroy, or suffer
to perish a thing that God made, and that had a
soul in it, and for whom I believe Christ died."

"Well, well, well !" shouted Mrs. Bryant, perfectly astounded at sentiments so unusual in that
age. "Heard ever any civilized body the likes of

that? Call a savage a fellow-creature! Talk about
nursing one of their brats! I wouldn't put it to
a cow, — no, nor to a breeding sow! I wouldn't
disgrace a hog so much. I suppose if an Indian
should come to your house, you would say, 'Take
all there is here, it is yours;' then lay your head
down on the door-step and ask him to cut it off."

"I should defend my land and property," said
Elizabeth, "for we bought our land and paid for
it; but I would be willing to buy it over again, if
I could have the names of the Indians that owned it
at the bottom of the title-deed. I believe the property would wear better. I'll shoot an Indian, if I
am called to, and when it is my life or his; but no
child of mine shall mangle an Indian after the
breath is out of his body, or take his scalp, or
murder an Indian woman or child, if I can hinder
it, let them do what they will to me or mine. And
I will feed them when they are hungry, and warm
them when they are cold, for I know that God
made them as well as me."

"O, you don't know them as well as we do,"
exclaimed all the rest in a breath; " we have summered and wintered them. They will eat your
bread, and cut your throat as soon as they are
done."

" Don't I?" she replied; and then related the
story of the Indian who brought the corn and meat,
while the tears sprang to her eyes as she recalled
the agony of that terrible winter.

13

What reply the auditors, who had presumed so much upon her ignorance of Indian character, would have made to this we know not, for Mrs. Bryant, looking at the hour-glass, which was almost run down, said that it was four o'clock, and time for her to be getting supper. Upon this they all volunteered to assist her. " O, no," said she, " it is all cooked. There is nothing to do except to make the tea."

" I hardly thought I could come," said Elizabeth, " I had so much to do getting ready to move into garrison; but when you sent me word that you had got some tea, I told Hugh I must and would come. Where in the world did you get it ? "

" Why, Mr. Bryant's brother sent it to us from Barnstable, — you know we came from the Cape. He piloted an English ship into Provincetown, and the Captain gave him some, — you know you can get such things there. We haven't had a drop before since we came here. You could always get it there by paying enough for it."

" We had some last Thanksgiving," said Elizabeth, " but I guess it will be a long day before we shall get any more, for I expect this Indian war will make us as poor as ever, if we escape with our lives. We were just beginning to raise crops and live comfortably."

CHAPTER IX.

CAPTURE OF REED.

AT half past four o'clock the men came in with their guns on their shoulders, and set them up in the corner of the room. Attracted by the sight, the children (who were quite sure to be present when least wanted) came crowding into the room, and began to finger the guns, causing Mrs. Bryant to exclaim, in sharp tones, " Let those guns alone, can't you! You'll be shot! 'Mr. Bryant, do see to that girl, — as I live, crawling up on those guns! ' "

Bryant took the child, which didn't mend matters much, as she instantly began to scream with all her might.

" Sarah Jane Bryant, do you take that child this minute, and get out of the house every soul of you! And do you stay till we are done supper, and you shall have some sweet-cake."

In the course of half an hour, hearing the child crying bitterly, Mrs. Bryant looked out; there it was, its clothes hitched to a stump, screaming and struggling to reach the rest of the children, who were so engaged in their original employment as to be entirely regardless of its screams.

Some of them were lying flat upon the ground, and, with sticks for guns, were taking aim at one who was picking ivory plums ; another, with a stick broken across to represent a tomahawk, was crawling up behind the screaming child. They had painted each other's faces with clay from the brook and smut from a stump, in black and blue stripes. Tim Cloutman, his head ornamented with a cock's tail-feathers, had thrown Abigail on the ground, where she lay as though dead, while he, his left hand twisted in her hair and his knee on her back, was, with a case-knife, going through the operation of scalping her, doing his best meanwhile to imitate the scalp-yell.

Stepping back, Mrs. Bryant beckoned to Mrs. Cloutman, who sat nearest the door, and bade her look.

" They have learned that from hearing us talk."

" God grant it be not a forerunner," was the reply.

The children's sport was cut short by the shrill voice of the mother: " Sarah Jane Bryant, what upon earth are you doing ? Don't you hear that child, you good-for-nothing jade, you ? "

" O ma'am ! " replied Sarah Jane, " we are play-ing Indian."

" I'll Indian you, if you don't take care of that

child! Here, give her to me. Now," (throwing them a cloth,) " go straight to the brook and wash yourselves! Pretty pickle you are in, — and company in the house."

Clutching the cloth, they ran to the brook, only to put on infinitely more dirt than they took off.

" Now supper is ready," said Mrs. Bryant, " but where are the folks? Where is William McLellan and my Stephen? Mrs. Cloutman, what has become of your man? He was here a minute ago."

Going to the door to call them, she found William and her son engaged in throwing the tomahawk, while Cloutman was sitting on a log looking at them. They had hewed a flat place on the side of a pine-tree, and marked an Indian's head on it with a piece of charcoal, and were trying to hit it. William hit it every time; but young Bryant, who was learning, could not half of the time hit the tree, and when he did he hit the handle or poll of the hatchet instead of the edge, so that it fell down without sticking in.

" I don't see how you do that, Bill," said Cloutman. " I don't believe I could do half as well as Bryant."

" You see it's all practice, Mr. Cloutman," replied William. " I can shoot an arrow or fling a tomahawk as well as any Indian between here and Canada, though they are bred and born to it as it were. You see a tomahawk will make so many turns in going such a distance; at so many paces it will

strike with the handle down, at so many with the
handle up.   At first you must pace off the distance,
but after a while you will get so as to measure it
with your eye ; you know there is a good deal of
judgment to be used in shooting with a rifle as to
distance.   It is a good deal like that."

"I wish," said Cloutman, as he came in, "I was
as good with a gun as I think Billy will be if he
lives.   If the Indians know their own interest, they
will kill him as soon as they can.   He'll make some
of their heads ache if he comes to be a man."

Indeed, if there is any truth in the old proverb,
that practice makes perfect, this prediction was in a
fair way to be verified, since from the time the boy
was seven years old, — when, with an old hoop for a
bow and a piece of mullein-stalk for an arrow, he
made a target of the oven-door, — he had practised
incessantly, either with the bow or the gun, and
latterly had killed nearly all the meat the family
had consumed.   He had also kept himself in powder
and lead by trapping beaver.

The supper being now on the table, all were invited (in the phrase of the day) to "sit along and
partake of such as we have."   After grace had been
said by Hugh, they all fell to with right good-will.

Bryant was in good circumstances for those times.
Not having to buy his land, as he was the son of one
of the Narragansett soldiers, he had been able to
stock his farm and hire some help in clearing it, and
to raise all the essentials of life in abundance.   Bry-

ant's furniture was much better than Hugh's, who
indeed could be scarcely said to have any worth
the name, and that little had been all made by
himself, whereas Bryant's had been brought from
Massachusetts. Instead of a cross-legged table, he
had one with leaves ; instead of stools, " boughten "
chairs with bottoms of basket-work. Mrs. Bryant
had a hair sieve, a case of drawers, a brass kettle,
and an iron mortar, while Elizabeth's mortar was
only a rock-maple stump. Yet Bryant treated
McLellan with great deference, and often sought
his advice, both out of respect to his character and
his position as an elder in the church, — perhaps
also from a secret consciousness that, with all his
disadvantages at the start, he was the better man of
the two, rapidly overcoming the distance between
them, and would eventually outstrip him in the
race for competence.

The food and the furniture of the table were quite
different from those in style at the present day.
The table-cloth was of fine linen, figured and woven
by Mrs. Bryant's own hands ; the plates, or, as they
were then called, trenchers, were square pieces of
wood dug out, and at least not liable to dull the
knives. Mrs. Bryant rejoiced in a china cup and
saucer, of very small size, and quite beautiful, which
was an heirloom, and given her by her grandmother,
who brought it from England. As for her company,
she having sent them word that she was to have
tea, they had brought cups and saucers and spoons

with them, as she had not enough for so many. The sugar-bowl was of pewter, and filled with maple sugar. In the centre of the table, in a tin dish, was an enormous chicken-pie, upon which Mrs. Bryant, who was proud of her cookery (as what good housewife is not?) had exerted all her skill. The crust was rich and flaky, of home-made wheat-flour, which Mrs. Bryant had sifted as fine as could be, with plenty of butter rolled into it; there were several circles, beginning at a little distance from the edge, and growing smaller and smaller as they approached the centre, all made of pastry. In the centre was a round hole through which the gravy most invitingly oozed, emitting a savory steam, that made Bose, who had come without invitation, lick his chops so as to be heard all over the room. The space between the edge of the dish and the first circle was filled with ornamental figures, which the good housewife had made with a trunk-key before baking. She then rolled out some dough, and cut out some stars and hearts, and put them into the second row, first a heart and then a star, and so on; then she took an acorn that had the cup on it, and pressed it into the dough all round the last row, and then put her completed work into the oven for baking. The pie was flanked by a custard pudding, some boiled pork, and a large dish of potatoes, which in that day were almost as great a rarity as oranges. In addition to this, there were loaves of Indian bread, and plates of butter, and a great bowl of stewed cranberries, sweetened with maple sugar, which are as good and fashionable now as they were then. The piles of provisions rapidly disappeared before these valiant " trenchermen," the pork and potatoes first, then the chicken-pie and the pudding.

The dishes being removed, Mr. Bryant placed on the table some pewter tankards and a gallon of milk-punch in a large wooden bowl made out of beech, and beautifully turned and ornamented on the outside with figures. " His Majesty's health, God bless him!" was then drunk, after which many compliments were paid to Mrs. Bryant for her cookery, which she received with evident pleasure, but due humility, saying by way of reply, " that she knew it was not just the time to have company, when they were so much pressed with work and danger at the door; but still she and William felt that it would be pleasant for the old neighbors, who had suffered so much hardship together, to meet sociably once more before they went into garrison, as it could never seem so home-like there."

" What do you think about going into garrison, neighbors ? " said Bryant. " I don't know but we are running too much risk; half of the families have fled, and the rest are all in the fort but us. The Captain was at my house this morning ; he says that he knows the Indians will be here soon, and thinks they are not far off now."

" He was down at our house," said Hugh, " urging me to go. But we might, as I told him, as well

be killed by the Indians, as go into the fort with
nothing in the ground, and starve to death after we
get there."

"It is just as the elder says," observed Cloutman. "A man can do more in one day on his place
when he and his family are living on it, than he
can in two when he is half a mile off. It is high
time the grain was in, and I am inclined, since we
have already risked so much, to stay out till we get
the grain in and the fences up."

"I," said Reed, "have got everything done except harrowing in a piece of grain ; I could go in
to-morrow, but I sha'n't go and leave the rest out.
I will help you get your work along, and we will all
go in together."

"I know a good deal about Indians," said Clout
man, "and I think some of 'em know me ; therefore I may say, without fear of being thought a
coward, that they are a terrible enemy. They will
creep through the woods with no more noise than a
fish in the water ; they will track any one they are
after, I sometimes think, like a hound, by the scent.
Though they have no great patience to besiege a
place, there is no end to the patience with which
they will dog a man till they run him down. When
we are at war with them no man can be sure, at any
hour of the day or night, that he is not covered by
an Indian's rifle, or that they are not prowling
around his dwelling. I suspect that they have some
scores to settle with me that they will try to square

up before this war is over. When I tended the old mill, at the lower falls, in 1741, an Indian got into the mill while I was gone to supper, and lay down behind the logs. Just before twelve o'clock, as I was setting the log, he pulled trigger at me, but his gun missed. I flung the crowbar with which I was setting the log at him, and knocked him down. Then I set the saw going, and put him on the log, and held him there till I split him in two, and flung the halves down the saw-pit. They never forget anything, and I think the sooner we can finish our work and get into the fort, the better. I haven't been used to think or care whether they had a grudge against me or not ; but since I have got this woman and little boy," (laying his hand kindly upon his wife's knee,) " I feel different."

" O, Edward ! " said his wife, " don't stay out another day ! It is better to be safe, if you do have to work at a little disadvantage."

" I think as much," said Bryant.

" But, William," replied his wife, " I can't get along in the fort without a cradle for this babe, and if you will take a day and make one, I will risk my scalp a day longer."

" These are troublous times, neighbors," said Hugh, " and should teach us our dependence. When we part we know not that we shall ever meet again. Shall we have a word of prayer before we separate ? "

" With all my heart," replied Bryant ; and these

iron men, with their wives and little ones, knelt reverently together before God.

The leave-taking occupied some time, as the women had a great many last words to say, and every one must needs kiss the baby. In the meantime the children, who were but seldom in each other's company through fear of the savages, began to anticipate the pleasure of being in garrison.

"Won't we have such a nice time!" said John Reed. "The stockade will keep off all the wind, and we can have our plays right under the lee of it in the warm sunshine. I seed it when they were building it, and I went up to carry father's dinner, — mother and me."

"Yes," said Tim Cloutman; "and there will be such a heap of boys there! — me, and John Reed, and Joe Harvey, and the Hamblens, and Jim Mosier, and Johnnie Watson, and the Bryants and McLellans. Won't it be nice?"

"They have got a drum up to the fort, and a flag-staff, — O just as high! — and a color. They are going to have the gun fired every night and morning, — my mother said so, — and it will scare the Indians awful, and they'll run clear to Canada."

"I seed them fire it one time," said Steve Bryant. "First it went fizz, fizz, and then bang! O my! what a noise!"

"Well," chimed in John Reed, "we can't have any chance to go fishing, or drown out woodchucks, or get beech-nuts or acorns."

" What of that ? " replied Tim. " They won't let me go now, because they say there's Indians round, and when they ain't round and I want to go beech-nutting or acorning, then they say that the bears are out beech-nutting and acorning. I'm sure I'd rather be in the fort, where there ain't any bears nor acorns either."

" Besides," said Abigail, " up at the fort are the nicest great large chips and blocks that the men cut off. We can build the nicest baby-houses, and have our babies in them ; and when Mrs. Bryant's little baby gets big enough, we will have that out there, and build a little house to put it in, and have our tame crow out there too. Jim Mosier has got a little kitten."

" Baby-houses ! " broke in the martial Tim. " Who cares for baby-houses ?   We'll have bows and arrows and guns, and build forts, and play French and English, have battles, and lick the Frenchmans," cried Tim, doubling both his fists in a heat of warlike excitement. Tim was eight years old.

Just as they set out, they heard in the woods behind the house the screams of a blue-jay, — a sound too common at that season of the year to attract much notice. Cloutman merely said, "There's a fellow, Bill, that will be wanting to pull up our corn one of these days."

The sun was still about an hour high, and they separated thus early on account of Indians, and because they had cows to milk before dark. Bose had already gone home to get up the cows.

They had passed over about a third of the distance between Bryant's and the spot where they were to separate from Cloutman, when a fir-bush, growing on the edge of the path behind them, began to wave, although there was not a breath of wind. At length from beneath its very roots appeared the glaring eyeballs and grim features of a savage in his war-paint, the rest of his body concealed by the roots of the bush and a heap of brush that lay around them. The subtle savages, uniting their strength, had pulled up the tree by the roots, with all the moss and earth adhering to it. After digging out the soft earth beneath with their hands, they had placed their comrade in the cavity thus formed, and replaced the tree, covering the whole with moss and brush so artfully that it had all the appearance of a growing tree. A little farther on the party came to a hollow log, the end of which protruded into the footpath ; across the end of this log Abigail caught her clothes so firmly that her father was obliged to stop and disentangle them. But no sooner had they passed on out of ear-shot, than from this very log crept a savage, armed with knife and tomahawk. The two savages, with a passage as noiseless as that of a bird, withdrew to the recesses of the forest, where they were joined by two others, who, like themselves, seemed to have sprung from the ground or fallen from the clouds. The screams

of the jay now ceased, the voices of the settlers died
away in the distance, the savages retired still farther
into the forest, and no sound was heard save the
low moan of the night-wind through the wilderness.

The Indians at this time obtained more from the
English for the ransom of prisoners, than the bounty
given by the French for English scalps; hence,
except when they had some grudge to satisfy, or
when the captives were wounded and therefore unable to sustain the fatigue of a journey to Canada,
or were children and too young to travel, or when
they themselves were pursued and could carry the
scalps easier than the captives, they seldom took
life, if they could without too great risk to themselves take prisoners. It was also Indian law that
the captives belonged to the one who seized them first.
Hence it was often the case that one savage would
seek to kill another's prisoner, if he had against him
any personal enmity; then the captor would defend
his prisoner, and sometimes bury his knife in the
breast of the other, not out of any feeling of compas-
sion for the captive, but because he did not wish to
lose his ransom. The Indians had found out that
the party were at Bryant's, and had determined, if
they were returning home unarmed, to ambush and
rush upon them with knife and tomahawk, kill and
scalp the children, and take the men and women
prisoners. To this end they had pushed over a
dead tree full of limbs that stood just ready to fall
beside the path, that, while the men were occupied

in removing it for the women and children to pass, they could spring upon them with advantage. They had therefore placed the Beaver, who, as being but a boy, was quite useless in a grapple with men, in the top of a large hemlock that commanded a view of Bryant's door, with orders, if the party were armed, to give the scream of a blue-jay.

As this proved to be the case, the Indians — who had a wholesome dread of the settlers' rifles, and especially of Cloutman, who, in addition to being extremely skilful with the rifle, weighed two hundred and twenty pounds, was in the prime of life, and of such strength that he could crush a walnut between his thumbs and a plank, and once carried nine bushels of potatoes in a bed-sack — determined to let them pass unmolested, and wait with Indian patience for a better opportunity.

Upon Friday night, the 18th of April (old style), 1746, the McLellan family, the day's work being ended, were all in the house. Hugh was sitting in the door, in order that he might have all the fast fading daylight for his work. Calling to William, he told him to take the pails and go to the spring and get a supply of water for the night.

The path to the spring was waylaid by Indians, who were in ambush behind the house, and who, as they afterwards said, could have touched him with their hands. They suffered him to pass unmolested, because they hoped when it became dusk to surprise the whole family. Many of them were the same Indians who had lived among the settlers, and knew their habits ; with these were some Canada Indians and a few Penobscots.

They knew that, in consequence of the log-house being dark, the family were accustomed, when it was pleasant, to sit with the door open till they went to bed, which was soon after dark, and then bar it for the night. Their plan was, as soon as it grew dusk, to steal round the corner of the house, and, before the door was barred, rush in. They would probably have succeeded, and surprised and overpowered Hugh, who was busily at work, before he could have reached his gun, which hung on hooks over the fireplace ; but their plan was frustrated by Bose, who, when he was ordered out doors for the night, went out before the door, stretched himself, and snuffing the air, ran back into the house growling and showing his teeth.

" Indians ! " exclaimed Hugh, shoving back his bench, shutting the door, and thrusting the awl he was at work with over the wooden latch.

In another moment William supplied a more efficient fastening by putting the handle of a broken skillet into an inch auger-hole that was bored for that purpose in the post above it. They then put in the additional bars provided for the purpose. They had a milk-pan full of powder, four guns, and plenty of lead, but it was not in balls. Elizabeth hung up a blanket before the fire, to keep the light

14

from being seen outside, and went to melting lead in a skillet, and running bullets with an iron spoon, while Hugh and William lay at the loop-holes with two guns apiece. But the night passed away without further alarm, the Indians having relinquished their attempt.

At sunrise they ate their breakfast, resolved to finish their work that day, and go into the fort the next morning. Just as they were about to start for the field, John Reed came to the door.

" Good morning, Elder."

" Good morning, John."

" I came down to see if you would lend me a chain."

" Yes; there it is in the crotch of that tree."

" I want to harrow my grain in, and go into garrison to-morrow."

" We had a little bit of a scare last night," said Hugh.

" Did you see any Indians ? "

" No ; but just as we were going to bed, Bose all at once ran into the house, and growled and stuck up his back, as he always does when there are Indians round. He always did hate an Indian. We fastened the house and kept watch, but saw and heard nothing more, and there are no tracks around the house. I think he smelt some wild creature. But William and his mother, who have noticed the dog's ways more than I have, are positive that it was Indians."

"I have not seen any Indian sign," said Reed, "and I have been in the woods a great deal, and I don't think there are any round; though, as Ed Cloutman said the other night, they are a critter to be felt before they are seen; and it seems a clear tempting of Providence to stay out any longer."

"Well, Mr. Reed," said William, "I've had that dog ever since he was a pup, and I've hunted with him months, and I may say years; I ought to know his ways by this time. Now he always hated an Indian, and before the war, when they used to be in and out of the house every day, and came to the door to grind their knives and tomahawks, he would have torn them to pieces if we would have let him. But after we beat him for it, when he smelt one of them coming he'd stick up his bristly hair, and growl, and put his tail between his legs, and go off growling into the house, and get under the bed or the table, and lie there and snarl till they were gone. He did just so last night, — didn't he, mother?"

"Yes," she replied, "and was uneasy for an hour, and then gave it up and went to sleep."

"Now," continued William, whose education in the woods had made him a real hunter, and who found a fruitful theme whenever he touched upon the good qualities of his dog, "it stands to reason it was Indians. If it had been a moose, or a bear, or a catamount, his tail wouldn't have been between his legs, I can tell you; but his tail would have been right up. Instead of growling he would have begun to whine and jump up on me, and kiss me, and have gone and looked up to the gun, and barked, and tried to coax me to go after it, whatever it was. Now Bose don't know we are at war with the Indians, and he thought if he barked he should be whipped, because we used to whip him when he barked at them, and so he showed his spite in the only way he dared to."

" Well," replied Reed, " I am hindering you and myself too. Mrs. McLellan, I'll thank you for a drink of milk."

He drank the milk, and, throwing the chain over his back, started for home. The milk made him dry, and when he came to the brook he flung the chain from his shoulder, and, putting down a piece of bark at the edge of the water to keep himself from the clay, spread out his hands on either side, and laid his breast on the bark to drink. Two Indians instantly threw themselves upon him, and, forcing his head and face into the water, mastered him. Forcing his hands behind his back, they bound them with thongs of deer-hide, and then helped him to rise.

As soon as he had regained his breath, and blown the mud and water from his nose and mouth, he exclaimed to one of the savages whom he knew, " What a mean, cowardly way that is to set upon a man! Let me loose, and if I don't handle you both I will go with you of my own accord."

" Indian no such big fool," was the reply. " Reed very strong man ; Indian hold him fast."

Reed administered a kick to the savage who stood before him, that sent him backward into the brook, which was running even with its banks. The other savage laughed at this, and, laying his hand upon his shoulder, said, " Come." Reed, well knowing that any hesitation would be followed by a blow of the tomahawk, sullenly obeyed. They took him through the woods, over his own land, and as they went he could hear the voice of William McLellan driving his oxen, but, as the Indians had taken the precaution to gag him, could give no alarm. Indeed, these Indians had started for Hugh's, but, hearing the click of the chain on Reed's shoulder, they gave up that part of their plan, and, concealing them-selves, fell upon him.

The Indians were very reluctant to fire a gun if they could kill or capture without, fearing to alarm the garrison. A band of scouts, with whom were three Saco Indians, had come from Saco the afternoon before, on their way to Windham, but had left that morning at daylight; whereas the Indians thought they were still at hand, and were fearful of bringing this large force upon them, especially as the friendly Indians who were with them could follow their trail. They were anxious to take Cloutman, and to obtain his rifle, which was an excellent one, as they well knew; and as for the Bryants, they hated them, and had many injuries to avenge upon them. Their antipathy to the Bryants was not only of long standing, — as his ancestors were engaged in Philip's war, and had inflicted much injury upon the Indians, — but it partook of a personal character, as in time of peace they had uniformly treated them with harshness, and refused to give to them when it was in their power.   But the day of reckoning had come, and the savage of all beings on earth was the least likely to be slack in repaying injuries.

CHAPTER X.

MASSACRE OF THE BRYANTS.

A S Cloutman was going into garrison, and must therefore leave his field to a great extent unwatched, he had bestowed extra labor on his fencing. The day before the occurrence we are about to relate he had " top-ridered " it all round with spruce-trees, leaving all the brush on them. This morning he was sowing grain, which was the last work he had to do before going into the fort.

The field was surrounded by woods in which the Indians had hidden themselves. Five of the strongest and most active concealed their guns in the woods, and, armed only with knives, prepared to grapple with him, and, if possible, take him alive, as they expected a large ransom, while the other three kept their arms, in order to shoot him rather than permit him to escape. Watching their opportunity, when his back was turned and he was sowing from them, they sprang towards him. Hearing the footsteps, he turned, and saw the great odds against him, and that they had got his rifle, which he had left at the end of the piece.

He instantly ran for Bryant's house; but when he came to the fence, which he had made so very high the day before, in attempting to leap it, he got tangled in the brush, and fell back. Once more he attempted it, with the same result. Cloutman was, like many men of great size and strength, deficient in agility. William McLellan or Bryant would have cleared it at a leap. Finding the Indians were upon him, he turned and faced them. He struck the first with his fist with such force as to break his jaw, felled the second with a back-handed blow, and, catching up the third, flung him senseless upon the ground, and put his foot upon his neck. As he had his back to the fence, he would doubtless (such were his enormous strength and courage) have got the better of the whole of them, had not the others, coming up, presented their guns at his breast; seeing that further resistance was useless, he surrendered. Had he not fenced his field so well, he would have got to the Bryants, and saved himself and them.

Bryant was an exceedingly active man, a great wrestler, and very swift of foot. He was wont to say that in a two-mile race he could outrun any Indian he ever saw. When the Indians came upon him, he, with his son, a lad of twelve years, was fencing, having no gun with him. He told his son to hide himself in the woods, while he ran for the garrison. The Indians, knowing Bryant would alarm the garrison, pursued him at their utmost speed; but he ran like a deer, and distanced them in a moment. Seeing that he would escape, one of them fired and broke his arm.

As he was obliged to hold up the shattered arm with the other, they now rapidly gained upon him, nearly exhausted with loss of blood and with his efforts. He had reached the bank of a little brook that skirted the high ground upon which the garrison was built; a little farther and he would be in safety. As he summoned his failing strength to leap the brook, he heard the footsteps of his relentless foes. In that terrible moment he caught sight of one of his neighbors, Daniel Mosier, coming down the hill from the garrison, with a loaded gun on his shoulder. " Fire, Daniel, for God's sake, fire ! " cried Bryant, with the energy of despair, as the footsteps of his pursuers came nearer.

But Mosier hesitated. A man of excellent capacity and character, and ever ready to do his part in all other respects, he yet lacked the nerve required to act up to the stern code of the settlers, which required every man to stand by his neighbor to the death. At the summons of Bryant, he levelled his rifle at the foremost Indian, who, seeing the motion, slacked his speed, which gave Bryant opportunity to leap the brook. In another moment he would have been in safety; but Mosier hesitated to pull the trigger. That hesitation was fatal to Bryant. The two savages — who were armed only with knife and tomahawk, having thrown aside their rifles to run —

saw it, and, leaping the brook, buried their weapons in his skull.   One of them then, placing his knee on the dead man's breast, and taking hold of the hair upon the top of the head, lifted the head up a little way from the ground ; he then made a circular cut with his knife around the roots of the hair, and, taking hold of the raw edge with his teeth, tore off the scalp.   It was the work of but an instant to him, made familiar with it by long practice.

Mosier returned to relate the tale to the inmates of the garrison, by whom his failure to fire was never either forgotten or forgiven.   As for the Indians, they hastened to join the rest in completing their work of vengeance at Bryant's house.

The boy ran through the woods for McLellan's, but, fearing that the Indians would overtake him, plunged into the brook, thrusting his head under the roots of a tree that grew on the edge of the bank, while his body was immersed to the neck, and concealed by the bank.   The Indians, coming to the brook and losing his track, did not search narrowly for him, as they were eager to plunder the house, and destroy the rest of the family.

Bryant, when he left home, had charged his wife to keep the children near the house, and not permit them to go ranging about in the woods.   In order to do this, she had promised them, if they would stay round the door, that they should have some maple syrup, and boil it down to sugar.   She had just gone down cellar, through a trap-door in the floor, to get

it for them, telling them, as they attempted to follow her, that if they didn't stay up-stairs they
shouldn't have a drop. Thus debarred from following, they all got down on their knees, at the
mouth of the hole, trying to peep down to see
where their mother put it, and what she kept it in,
and how much she had. Thus the doomed family
were all together on the floor.

Scarcely had she disappeared in the cellar, when
the savages, finding the door unfastened, rushed
into the room. The children at the sight of these
demons set up a cry of horror; the mother thrust
her head up the trap, when she beheld the chief of
the band, a gigantic savage, his hands red with
blood, and the scalp of her husband at his belt.
He instantly slammed the door down upon her
head, and stood on it, while the rest proceeded to
the work of slaughter.

Maddened by the screams of her children, per-
ishing beneath the tomahawks of the savages, the
mother made frantic efforts to lift the door, but in
vain. In a few moments the cries ceased. The
door was thrown open, and the mother beheld the
elder children mangled and scalped, lying in their
blood upon the floor. While the miserable woman
gazed upon this heart-rending sight, an Indian, in
whom she recognized the one upon whom more than
a year before she had flung the hot suds, was in the
act of drawing the babe from its cradle by the feet;
swinging the little creature around his head, the

cruel monster dashed out its brains against the stone jambs of the fireplace, and threw it on the bed. With a mother's instinct the poor woman rushed to the bed, caught the mangled form in her arms, and pressed it to her bosom.

While she was thus engaged, the chief whose prisoner she was, passing a thong of deer-skin over her arms, pinioned them to her side. No sooner was this done, than the savage who had destroyed the babe, snatching it from her grasp, flung it into a kettle of boiling water that hung over the fire, exclaiming in hellish glee, "Hot water good for Indian dogs, good for pappoose too." He then danced before her, snapping his bloody fingers in her face, and, pointing to the bloody scalp at his companion's belt, assured her it was that of her husband. He then raised his hatchet to cleave her skull; but it was instantly wrested from his hand by the big Indian, who, enraged at this attempt to rob him of his captive, flung the other with great violence against the wall of the house. The Indians were very fond at this period of taking female captives, whom they sold for servants into French families; and as our grandmothers were excellent housewives, they were always in request in Quebec and Montreal. The Indians now ransacked the house, and, taking the guns, powder, and bullets, with what provisions they could carry, the wretched mother, and the fresh scalps of her butchered household, they hurried to the woods.

Meanwhile, the McLellans were busily at work. William, with one gun upon his shoulder and another fastened to the top of the yoke, drove the cattle and harrowed in the grain which his father scattered upon the smoking furrows of the virgin soil, filled with fertilizing ashes and the mould of decayed forests. The birds sang overhead, and the robins followed the harrow to pick up the grubs and worms which it dislodged from the dead bark of the old stumps, and all seemed peaceful and propitious. The children and their mother were no less busy at home. Elizabeth was sitting in the door, spinning linen thread. The children were making a garden in the sun at the door; Abigail was digging up the ground with a hoe, and Mary with a butcher-knife. Alexander had fastened one of his father's shoes to Bose's tail, and was pulling him by the neck and trying to make him draw it along. But all Bose would do was to wag his tail back and forth, and thus twitch the shoe from one side to the other, licking the child's face between-whiles.

"Mother," cried Abigail, "do make Cary come into the house; he keeps getting right on to my hoe, so that I can't plant my beans."

"Ma, I can't hoe one mite!"

Just as Elizabeth rose from her wheel to see to the children, she heard the report of the gun that was fired at Bryant. She then told Abigail to go up to Bryant's and see what that gun was fired for. Now there was nothing Abigail loved better than to go to Bryant's and get with their children. But she remembered the alarm of the last night and was afraid to go, and went and hid in the brush. After some time had passed, her mother, finding she had not been, boxed her ears, and sent her off. The little girl went on her way, but reached the house just after the Indians had gone. She heard them talking in the woods as they went.

As she came up to the house, Sarah Jane, whom the Indians had scalped and left for dead, lay right in the door, with her raw and bloody head sticking out at it. She knew Abigail, and in a faint voice asked her to give her a drink of water. But the child was too much frightened to heed; she ran for home, and when she reached there fainted at the threshold. Her mother put her on the bed, and threw some cold water in her face. She revived, said "Indians," and fainted again. Elizabeth instantly blew the horn, barred the doors, and loaded the two guns that were in the house.

The moment the sound of the horn was heard in the field, William, reaching over the shoulder of the nigh ox, unhooked the chain, and, without stopping to unyoke them, he and his father seized their guns, and ran for the house. When they reached the house, they found it fastened, and Elizabeth at the loop-hole with a gun. The child by this time was able to tell what she had seen. They knew not but the garrison was surprised, and all in it, together with the other neighbors, killed. They drew water, filled all their vessels, and prepared for a siege. " If they master our scalps," said Hugh to his son, " they shall cost them dear, and not while this powder holds out."

The men in the garrison had been told by Mosier of Bryant's slaughter ; but being few in number, and not knowing how great the force of the Indians might be, they remained within the walls, only firing the alarm gun to warn the neighboring garrisons that there were Indians around.

The McLellans kept watch that day and the following night. At noon the next day a body of men were seen coming over what is now called the Academy Hill. At first they took them for Indians, and prepared themselves for an attack ; but they proved to be rangers from Portland going to the fort. They had heard the alarm gun, and hastened to the rescue.

They came to the house, where they were gladly welcomed. William went to the field, and found the oxen feeding near where they had been left. Loading their things on a drag, they then went to the garrison. They now, with the inmates of the fort, began to investigate the fate of their neighbors.

Proceeding to Bryant's house, they found the dead body of the eldest daughter still lying in the doorway, over the sill of the door, whither she had crawled in her death-agony, perhaps in the vain attempt to follow her mother. The Indians had taken the blankets from the beds, and what bread

was baked, and left the marks of their bloody fingers on the milk-shelves that Mrs. Bryant had taken
so much pride in keeping as white as soap and sand
could make them. "By the living God!" exclaimed
Edmund Phinney, "if we don't revenge this accursed
butchery, we don't deserve the name of men."

They found the body of Bryant lying on the side
of the brook, and not finding that of Mrs. Bryant
or Stephen, concluded that they had been carried
away captive. In Cloutman's field, they saw the
marks of a desperate struggle, but found no blood.
At the brook, they found the chain Reed had flung
from his shoulder, and in the mud evident traces of
his struggle. While they were looking at the trail,
Bose, who had been shut up in the fort, came tearing
through the woods, and in an instant rooted out
from among the leaves an Indian belt, part of Reed's
shirt that had been torn off in the scuffle, and a
bunch of deer-skin thongs.

"That dog," said Captain Bean, the leader of the
rangers, looking on with admiration, "is worth his
weight in gold. What will you take for him, my
boy?"

"Sell Bose!" cried William. "I would as soon
sell my soul."

"It is as plain as day now," said the Captain.
"They waylaid Reed here, and bound him: these
are some of the thongs that they left; and they
have taken Cloutman, and Bryant's wife, and the
oldest boy, and made tracks for Canada. I believe
this dog will find their trail."

"That he will," said William. "He would track a humming-bird from one thistle to another."

They instantly put Bose on the trail, and he tracked them to the place where they had collected their captives; they saw the footprints of Reed, Cloutman, and Mrs. Bryant, but not of the boy; they therefore concluded that he had been shot in the woods. But while they were debating about it, he made his appearance. Bose led them to the bank of Little River, where the trail was lost. It was evident that they had here entered the water, which threw the dog off the scent; and as it was now dark, they were obliged to relinquish the pursuit for the night.

With the dawn of day, the rangers were on the track. The whole forenoon was consumed in regaining the trail, so artfully had it been concealed by the savages. It was then manifest that they had too much the start to be pursued with any hope of rescuing the captives, and the pursuit was reluctantly abandoned. Deep and general was the sympathy manifested when Stephen Bryant was brought by the scouting party to the fort. The poor boy had remained up to his neck in mud and water till nearly dark. He then crept from his hiding-place, and concealed himself in a hollow tree that grew near the bank of the brook, where he remained till he recognized the voices of William and Hugh among those who were searching for Reed.

As he stood amongst them, pale, covered with

15

mud and the rotten wood from the tree, which stuck to his wet clothing, his face scratched with briers, and bearing the traces of recent tears, every heart yearned over him.

"Have the Indians gone?" was the first question of the bewildered boy, upon whose mind the impress of those horrid forms still remained vivid.

Being told that they were gone, he then said, "I want to go home; I want to see my mother."

At this declaration there was not a dry eye among the inmates of the fort, who, from the youngest to the oldest, were grouped around him.

"Your mother is not there," at length said Elizabeth, "the Indians have taken her to Canada."

"Did they kill my father?"

"Yes."

"I was afraid they had; I heard the gun when I was running through the woods. Where are my brothers and sisters?"

"They are dead."

"Where is the baby?"

"That is gone, too."

"Did mother carry it with **her?**"

"No; the Indians killed it."

"The little baby?"

"Yes."

"Then I've no father, mother, brothers, or sisters. There's no place for me to go to, and nobody to take care of me," said the desolate boy, bursting into tears.

" God bless you, you poor little soul, you ! " cried Elizabeth, taking him into her motherly lap and kissing the tears from his cheeks, while her own fell fast and mingled with his. " I'll be a mother to you ; we'll all be your mothers ! You shall come and live with us, and as long as God gives me a crust you shall have half of it ! ''

Elizabeth now set herself to provide some food for him, as he was nearly famished, having been two days without eating. In the meantime Daniel Mosier's wife washed his face, and washed and combed out his hair, which was all matted together, and filled with mud and leaves and dust from the rotten tree, for he had lost his cap in running from the Indians. She then put some clean clothes of her son James on him.

While he was eating, Abigail drew her mother on one side, and asked her if she might give Stephen her tame crow. She said he felt so bad she wanted to give him something. There was nothing Abigail valued so much as her crow, and she knew no other way of showing her sympathy.

His hunger being satisfied, Hugh took him by the hand, and led him to view the remains of his father and brothers and sisters, which, having been cleansed from blood and filth, were laid out in one of the flankers. They then put the poor child, worn out with fright, sorrow, and fatigue, to bed ; and as he seemed afraid of being left alone, Mrs. Mosier lay down with him, and soothed him till he fell asleep.

The stern necessities of their situation left the settlers little time for grief or despondency. Their crops must be put in, and the Indians, made bold by success, would doubtless return as soon as they had disposed of their captives, and received the bounty for their scalps. The government now furnished them with eleven soldiers to assist in procuring food and defending the garrison. These soldiers, dressed in Indian fashion, were armed with rifle, tomahawk, and scalping-knife, and were most of them old hunters, accustomed to Indian fighting, and eager for Indian scalps, for which the government gave a bounty. They had a corporal of their own, and were under the command of Captain Phinney. A good part of their time was employed in scouting through the woods, in order to keep the Indians at bay, while the people were at work in their fields.

The men now labored in squads; they would all go to one field and hoe the corn, or gather the harvest, and then to another, being thus so strong in numbers, part keeping watch while the others worked, and all having their arms with them, as to bid defiance to the Indians.

The restless savages, secreting themselves in the woods in such a manner as to clude the vigilance of the scouts, prowled around the garrison, watching the opportunity, when the men were at work and the soldiers away, to get in and kill the women and children. Some two months after the attack on Bryant's family, Elizabeth and Mrs. Watson were bringing water from the spring to wash, the men being away at work; as the gate to the stockade was heavy, they left it open when they went in, not closing it till they came out again. All at once Bose, who was asleep in the sun before the gate, jumped up, ran into the yard, and began to growl; Elizabeth, who had just taken up the pail to go after another "turn," instantly pushed to the gate and fastened it. "There are Indians round," she said to her companion; "we shall have to do without water to-day."

"Perhaps he smells some wild creature," replied Mrs. Watson; "the woods are full of them."

"What is it, old dog?" said Elizabeth; "Indians?"

Bose at the word "Indians" drew back his lips and showed all his teeth, looking ugly enough. "There, I don't want any plainer language than that! Let us go up in the watch-box. They saw the gate open, and meant to get in. If they come near enough, I'll shoot one of them."

The two women went up to the watch-box over the flanker, and looked long and patiently. At length Elizabeth said, "See that bush move; there is an Indian behind that bush."

"It is the wind," said Mrs. Watson.

"There is no wind," was the reply.

"Perhaps the cattle are rubbing against it."

At that moment an Indian rose and peeped cau. tiously over the bush, looking at the fort. Mrs.

Watson gave a little scream, but it was drowned in
the report of the gun Elizabeth fired.   The men
were soon at the fort; she went with them to the
bush, behind which a large pool of blood was found,
and a trail showing that the savage had been carried
off by his companions.

That night Captain Phinney's old " line-backed "
cow and a heifer did not come home with the rest
of the cattle.   The next morning Edmund Phinney
went to look after them.   The Indians, who had
killed the cattle, fired upon him, breaking his left
arm, and wounding him in two other places.   Getting behind a tree, he took his gun in his right hand,
and, by retreating from one tree to another, kept
them at bay till a party who had heard the firing
came out from the fort to meet him.   There was no
doctor in the fort, and, wounded as he was in three
places, Eliphalet Watson and a hunter by the name
of Thorn went on foot to Portland with him to have
his wounds dressed.

During the following years the settlers were gradually reduced to the greatest distress for bread and
clothing.   It was so dangerous working the land,
and so much time was consumed in guarding against
the Indians, that they could raise but little.   Sometimes there was not more than two quarts of boiled
wheat in the fort.   The Indians burnt up the mill,
and they had to pound all their corn in a mortar, and
boil their grain, and eat it so.   Their oxen and cows

were killed, and as they were not able to plough
their old fields, nor to keep down the weeds and
sprouts from the stumps, but were obliged to raise
crops on burns (since they could do that after a
fashion without cattle), the fields went back in a
great measure to a state of nature, and their hay-
crop was nearly destroyed. They were obliged, at
the greatest peril of life, to resort to hunting for
food, and to clothe themselves with the skins of
beasts, and all, from the highest to the lowest, wore
moccasins. Hugh and Elizabeth, no novices in the
school of adversity, resorted to all their old expedients for procuring food, and she, laying aside her
wheel, began again to dress deer-skins.

At this period, his father and the rest having gone
to hunt, William was hoeing corn alone. Leaning
his gun against a stub some ten feet high at the
corner of the piece, he began to hoe the outside
row, next to the bushes. Casting a look at the other
end of the row, he saw through the bushes the face
of Conuwass, one of his Indian playfellows. He
then began to hoe backwards, as if to do his work
better, till he got the stub between him and the Indian ; then, seizing his gun, he crawled behind a
windfall, and lay in ambush, with his finger on the
trigger. Presently the Indian came creeping through
the bushes that skirted the edge of the corn, to the
foot of the stub, and, rising cautiously up, looked
around it, exposing a good part of his body. William instantly fired, calling out at the same moment,

"Conuwass, you no shoot young Bill this time!'
The Indian, clapping his hand on the wound, ran
into the woods, exclaiming, " Bill, you shoot him
well this time." The good old gun-barrel with which
William shot the Indian is now in the possession of
Colonel Hugh D. McLellan of Gorham.

The settlers, continually harassed by the Indians,
who were spread over the whole frontier, from the
Kennebec to Wells, cleared a large field on Bryant's
and Cloutman's lands, which they planted and sowed
in common. In the middle of this great field, out
of gun-shot from the woods or the log fence, they
raised their crops. Here also they made a breastwork of logs, behind which they might take shelter
if the Indians should attack them in force.

In the middle of this breastwork stood a large
stump, upon which they placed two boys, a little
and a big one, back to back, as sentries. The guns
were set up against the breastwork, over one corner
of which was a bark roof as a shelter in case of a
shower, and to keep the guns dry. The boys were
relieved every hour, a half-hour glass placed on the
top of the breastwork serving to divide the time.
Some of the boys who were lazy, and had rather
keep guard than hoe, were not very prompt about
turning it.

Foiled by this arrangement, the savages at length
hit upon a plan, the ingenuity of which was only
equalled by its audacity. Within twenty feet of

The Sentries.   Page 232.

the gate of the breastwork was a large rock, the northwest side of which was perpendicular, and about breast-high. Some half-burnt logs had been set up endways against this, one end of which rested against the top of the rock, the other on the ground. Small stumps and brush had been from time to time flung upon this in clearing the land, and among these rotting logs, blackberry and gooseberry bushes had grown up, completely darkening the cavity underneath. Into this hole four Indians had crept during the latter part of the night, their bodies naked to the breech-clout, and painted with smut and bear's grease, the better to harmonize with the burnt logs and brands among which they lay, and armed only with knife and tomahawk. Their plan was, when the sun became hot, and the boys tired and sleepy, to seize the moment when the men were all at the other end of the piece, with their backs to the stump, to rush upon the boys and tomahawk them. Then, raising the war-whoop, they would seize the guns and keep the unarmed settlers at bay till the rest, who were concealed in the woods, should reach the spot. They had also ambushed the path to the fort, as they supposed that the settlers, finding their foes in possession both of their arms and fortress, would flee to the garrison. It seemed that most, if not all, of this devoted band must now fall a sacrifice to the subtlety of their implacable foes, when the plot was made to recoil upon its authors by one of those trifling circumstances termed fortunate, but attributed by our pious ancestors to the special providence of God, at the very moment set for its execution.

CHAPTER XI.

BATTLE WITH THE INDIANS.

THE June morning dawned beautifully; the settlers, leaving the rangers to protect the garrison, came, men and boys, to their work. Placing their dinners, and a pail of water, beside the pine stump, they freshened the priming of their guns, and, leaning them against the wall of the breastwork, plied their labor.

That morning, William McLellan, who was now eighteen, and James Mosier, who was much younger, were put upon the stump as sentinels, — William on the side next to the rock, James on that next to the men, who, with their backs to the rock, were nearly at the other end of the piece. The sun was getting hot, and the boys began to grow sleepy. It had been some weeks since they had been alarmed by Indians, and in that field they felt quite secure. William, with his hands on the muzzle of his gun, and his chin upon his hands, was almost dozing. The Indians, whose keen eyes were fastened upon the boys, were preparing for a spring, and had already loosened their tomahawks in their belts, when James exclaimed, "Bill, here comes the Captain!"

They straightened themselves up, and brought their guns to a "shoulder-arms" as he came near. Thirsty with his work, he had come in quest of water.

"James," said he, after he had drank, "give me your gun, while you put that water where it will keep cool. It is going to be a very hot day, and it will be as warm as dish-water if it stays there. Put it under the side of that big rock, and be sure and set it level, for, if it is spilt, it will take one man to go after more, and two more to guard him."

This was a trying moment for the Indians, as James was approaching the very place of their ambush; but, with that unrivalled self-command which the savage possesses, they remained without the motion of a muscle, trusting that the bright glare of the sun without would so dazzle the eyes of the boy as to prevent him from seeing them in their dark retreat, especially as the color of their bodies harmonized so perfectly with the charred logs under which they lay. James placed his pail by the side of the rock; but as it was nearly full, and the ground fell off, he began to hunt for a stick or stone to put under the side of the vessel. In thus doing he looked into the hole, and his eyes encountered those of an Indian.

With a yell that reached the ears of the men at

the other end of the field, he tumbled over backwards, and, clapping both hands to his head, as if to save his scalp, uttered scream upon scream. The Indians, hatchet in hand, sprang over the body, and, hurling their weapons at their foes to confuse their aim, turned to flee. The guns made a common report, and two of the savages fell dead, when Captain Phinney, catching a musket from the wall, brought another down with a wound in the hip. The remaining savage, catching up the screaming boy, flung him over his back as he ran, thus shielding himself from William's fire, (who had provided himself with another gun,) as he was afraid of hitting his comrade. The moment he was out of gunshot, he flung down his burden, and fled to the shelter of the woods. The wounded savage was dispatched by a blow from the breech of Captain Phinney's rifle. James, now relieved from his fears, had screamed himself so hoarse that he made a noise much like a stuck pig in his dying moments.

"Now, William," said Captain Phinney, patting him on the shoulder, for he loved the boy, "you have shown yourself a man to-day, and one that is to be trusted. You know I have always said that you were more than half Indian. Now I want you to change clothes with that Indian I knocked on the head. I am going to send you to the fort, and I want your clothes to dress him in, and put him on the stump; for if these cunning imps miss any of us, they will know we have sent word to the fort. I want to take them in their own trap."

William put on the Indian's breech-clout, belt, and leggings, with knife and tomahawk. They then dressed the Indian in William's clothes, and, lashing him to a stake, set him on the stump, putting Stephen Bryant with him.

"Neighbors," said Captain Phinney, "these risky devils didn't come here without support near at hand. There are more, and a good many more, close by. I will say this for them, their plot was well and bravely laid, and nothing but the providence of God hindered its success. In my opinion, they won't give it up so, but they will ambush us as we go home to-night. We must therefore match craft with craft, if we can. William," continued he, "I want you to crawl to the fort and tell the corporal what has taken place here; that we shall come to the fort by the old road, with the sun just half an hour high, and that we expect to find the path waylaid. Tell him to take his men and try to come at that time upon the Indians' rear, and to be very careful that he is not ambushed himself."

They now took their hoes, and, putting William between Edmund Phinney and Hugh, the two largest men, the rest crowding round, that, if the Indians were watching from the woods, they might not see him, escorted him to the end of the piece, where, flinging himself flat on the ground, he crawled through the grass to the woods, made his way to the garrison, and delivered his message.

No sooner did William, after he had thus provided

for the welfare of the rest, find himself at leisure,
with a good part of a June day on his hands, than
his fancy was fired with the idea of discovering the
Indian ambush, — an act of cool daring, in one so
well acquainted with the keen senses of the savage,
which cannot be easily paralleled. Taking from the
Indian's girdle a bladder filled with paints, he got
one of the rangers to paint his body and face a
copper color, and tied up his hair in Indian fashion.
He did this in order that his color might be more in
harmony with the logs and trunks of the trees, and
thus he would not be so easily seen in the dusk
of the forest, and, if seen by the savages, might be
taken for one of their number. He now set out
upon his " war-path," to all appearance as veritable
a savage as ever swung a tomahawk. He proceeded
in the direction of the field till he judged himself
in the neighborhood of the Indians, and then, climb-
ing a hemlock, sat in the branches to watch the
crows.

Crows are singular birds ; they have a keen scent
for carrion, and are therefore always ready to hover
about an Indian camp, to pick the bones of the
game they kill. They are also a prying, meddle-
some thing, wanting to know all that is going on in
the world, and thrusting their noses into everybody's
business. I don't blame them for screaming when
they see a blue-jay, or a raccoon, because they steal
their eggs ; but if a fox is going along, or a man,
though it is none of their business, they will hover

over him and scream. Even the sight of a man
sitting still in the woods will attract their attention.

William knew this very well, for he knew all
about crows. He knew, too, that the crows had
young ones in their nests, not far from the road to
the field ; that, if the Indians were there, the crows
would be uneasy ; and that the very silence of the
Indians, and any attempt to hide in the woods,
would make these keen-sighted and wary birds uneasy, because they would suspect some design upon
them. He had not been long in the tree before he
heard the crows screaming, and saw two of them fly
towards a brook that skirted the road to the corn-
field, and shortly fly back to the spot from which
they started, and seating themselves on the top of a
dead pine, remain quiet.

He now made up his mind that the Indian ambush
was near the foot of that tree, — that some of the
Indians had gone to the brook to drink, and the
crows had borne them company. " These crows are
expecting a meal to-night," said William to himself ;
" I trust they will feast on Indians."

Fully alive to the deadly peril he incurred in
attempting to creep to an Indian ambush, the young
man, as we must now call him, bent all his faculties
to the work. As the brook had shelving banks, and
was then quite a stream, though now not worth the
name, and would lead him near to the spot where
he thought the Indians had gone to drink, he determined to take to the brook. The banks of the

brook would also shelter him from the notice of the crows, which might betray him to the Indians; for he knew that the Indians understood crow language better than he did. The brook also made a good deal of noise running over logs and roots, which would prevent his steps from being heard.

In the first place, he covered his head and neck with brakes and moss, so as not to be distinguishable from the vegetation around him. He then got into the brook, and with the greatest care proceeded in the direction of the dead pine. Presently he heard the cry of a crow; sinking still lower in the water, he pressed himself under the edge of the bank; his ear caught the crack of a dry stick, and in the next moment the savage who had escaped from the corn-field came to the brook. Filling a small birch-bark dish with water, he retired, evidently taking the water to others. In this savage, William now recognized the Beaver. "I am now on the 'war-path' as well as he," thought William, "and we will soon know which is the better man."

Within a few rods of him, an enormous pine, that grew on the bank of the brook, had been turned up by a hurricane, tearing up with its roots the soil for many rods, and breaking down in its fall many other trees, whose trunks lay across it in every direction, while blackberry and raspberry bushes had taken root in the decayed trunk; the wild ivy also, and the fox-grape, that grows in low places, had run over the limbs of the old tree like an arbor, leaving be-

16

tween them and the earth a large space, as the tree
lay up some six feet from the ground at its butt.
Thus there was a natural covered way, formed by
this mass of underbrush, from its root to nearly its
top.   Creeping through between two of the great
roots, from which the earth had fallen into the
brook, William made his way to the top of the tree,
when, looking through the brush, he beheld the ambush.   The Beaver was sitting with his back against
a tree, eating parched corn from his pouch; the rest
were asleep.   They were within less than a gunshot
of the road from the cornfield, waiting till the settlers should return from their work.

Departing with the same caution, William returned
to the fort.   The rangers, who had eaten their supper, were ready to set out.   " Now, my brave lad,"
said the corporal, " you know the ground, — lead on.
Place us where you please, and when you want us
to fire, just give the war-whoop."

William placed the corporal and part of the men
at a little distance from the tree, to annoy the Indians in their flight, while with the rest he crept
under the trunk of the old tree, and then patiently
watched their sleeping foes.   The sentinel now
aroused his fellows, who, freshening the priming of
their guns, crept behind the trees, which, concealing
them from the view of any one approaching by the
path, exposed their naked backs — which, newly
greased, shone in the rays of the sunlight slanting
through the leaves — to the deadly aim of their foes.

The click of the Indians' gun-locks was now heard, as they cocked their pieces. Presently the crows announced the coming of the settlers. William, unnoticed by the rest, shook the priming from his rifle, and then said to his comrades, " Leave the sentinel to me, — I have some old scores to settle with him."

The Indians now put their guns to their faces, and while their attention was thus entirely occupied in front, the rangers embraced the opportunity to cock their rifles, and thrust them through the brush for a sure aim. The heads of the settlers were now seen as they came cautiously along. But before the Indians could pull a trigger, the war-whoop rang through the arches of the forest, and the bullets, at short range, rattled into their tawny hides. William's rifle sent forth the bright sparks from the flint, but no report followed. " I am even with the Beaver now," said he; " I have spared his life, as he did mine. He said if his people knew that he had spared me, they would blush. I guess if the rangers knew that I shook the priming from my rifle, they would shoot me on the spot."

The remaining savages, rushing forward to escape the fire in their rear, encountered that of the corporal's party and of the settlers. Ten lay dead; the others, many of whom were wounded, fled. William was gratified to perceive that the Beaver was not among the slain, whom the rangers were now scalping.

While they were thus occupied, he ran to the garrison, and, taking Bose, overtook them before they had proceeded far on the trail of the flying foe. Aided by the dog, which followed the trail with unerring sagacity, they made great progress, and before they reached the river overtook two of the wounded, one of whom, entirely crippled, had hid himself in the bushes; the other could with difficulty walk, but, determined to sell his life dearly, took a tree, and menaced the party with his rifle. The rangers would soon have dispatched them both, but William begged their lives. He represented to them that Mrs. Bryant and many captives from Saco, Topsham, and Scarborough were in the hands of the French, and might be exchanged for them. The corporal seconding his request, in consideration of his services that day, they gave him the lives of both. As the moon shone bright, the rangers determined to follow the trail till midnight, and then camp on it, and pursue the next day, as they were in hopes, if they did not overtake the party, to pick up some wounded Indians, and obtain a few more scalps. Bose, at the command of William, and nothing loath, went with the rangers.

William's first care, when left alone with the savages, was to bind them with withes, which he cut from a beech and twisted. He then asked them if Beaver was wounded, and found to his great satisfaction that he was not. He now peeled some birch-bark from a tree, and, slitting the corners, turned

them up in the form of a dish. He then pinned
them together with a thorn, luted the joints with
clay, and gave his prisoners drink, after which,
putting some brush under their heads, he returned
to the garrison.

When he reached the fort, told the story, and
asked for aid to bring the wounded men to the
garrison, the greater part advised him to go back
and knock them on the head, and take their scalps;
and were only prevented from doing it themselves
by the remonstrances of Hugh and his wife, and
from the more weighty argument that they might
be exchanged for friends in captivity. "The mur-
dering, bloodthirsty vagabonds!" said those who
were in favor of killing. "When did they ever
spare the mother, or the child at her breast? See
what they did at Bryant's, — took that little dear
babe by the feet, and dashed out its brains before
the mother's eyes. Mrs. Bryant told Cloutman all
about it in Canada, and he wrote home to his wife."

"Yes," said Stephen Bryant, "and I should like
to cut their throats for them."

"What," said Watson, "did they do to the man
they took at New Meadows? They roasted him
alive at a slow fire, cut holes in his flesh, put in gun-
powder, then stuck him full of pitch-wood splinters,
and set him on fire."

"What did they do to my cousin?" said Hamblen.
"They stripped him naked, and tied him in a swamp
to be stung to death by mosquitoes, and every day
whipped him with nettles till he died."

" Besides, if their wounds are not dressed," said Edmund Phinney, " they will mortify this hot weather; and I should like to know who is going to do that ? "

" I would as soon touch a live rattlesnake," exclaimed Mrs. Watson.

" Well, I will," said Elizabeth, her spirit rising with the emergency, when she found them all against her. " I'll take care of any of God's creatures that are in distress. He has preserved me and mine. I'll not forsake the helpless, especially after the great mercy we have this day experienced."

" Well," said Jacob Hamblen, " I have some rights in this garrison, and I for one protest against Indians being brought into it. It was built to keep out Indians, not for a hospital to nurse them. If any want to live with Indians, let them go into the woods. We don't want *Irish* to tell us our duties. As the Scripture says, ' This one fellow came in to sojourn, and he will needs be a judge.' "

" Hear to this cock of the midden! " said Elizabeth, her eyes flashing, and using broad Scotch, as she was apt to do when her temper was up. " How brawly he crows whar there is no danger! No mair Irish than yourself, since our forbears came from Inverary, and we are lineally descended frae Mac-Callum More himself. It's weel kenned we are no people of yesterday, though it's but little I care for sic vanities. But just to let you ken that we belang to a race that hae been accustomed to hold their ain gear at the edge of the claymore, and I trow we are nae bastards —"

" Whist, whist, gude wife," interrupted her husband, " ye hae said enough, and mair than enough. Well, neighbors," he continued, turning to the excited group, " if we maun differ in our opinions, let us do it in such a manner as shall bring no discredit upon our calling as Christians, nor be displeasing to Him who has this day so signally appeared in our behalf. You will excuse me for saying that we also have some right in this garrison, as I think I furnished more labor than any person here, and that you could not have well built it without me, at least in the shape it is in now. But as neither I nor my family can in conscience consent either to butcher these poor creatures, or let them perish in the woods, we will leave the fort and go to our own house, and there we will take the Indians and take care of them, and when they recover, if they do recover, we will take them to Portland, and deliver them up to be exchanged ; and if we perish for our humanity, and in the way of duty, the Lord's will be done ! "

No pen can describe the astonishment of the company at this audacious proposal, uttered without a particle of passion, and in the tone of ordinary conversation. " It's just like yourself, Hugh," exclaimed his wife. " I knew you would say so. We risked our scalps to get a living, and we'll never be backward to do the same in the way of duty." Then turning to the rest, with all the indomitable pride of her Highland blood flashing in her eyes, she said: "We have nae the misfortune to be born in the country, but we came of gentle blood, and can afford to be generous. If you are attacked, send for us. We are three good rifles, not counting the children and the dog. Come, William, get the horse, and take them to the house. I'll be down with food and bandages."

The moment Elizabeth ended, Captain Phinney said: "Neighbors, will you permit this? I know we have suffered dreadfully from the Indians, but they have had their provocations. Something is certainly to be allowed for their ignorance, their lack of the Gospel, and their mode of life for ages. Don't let us, with the Gospel in our hands, be savages too. These people are new to the country; they have not, like us, been brought up to believe that the Indians are to be killed like wolves. Therefore I think that, being without our prejudices, they are more likely to be right in this matter than we. No one would think of letting a French prisoner die of his wounds; yet the French are more to blame for these cruelties than the Indians. The Indians did not want to go into this war, but they coaxed them into it, and hire them to fight against us. Don't let our brethren, who surely are not backward to strike when peril comes, go out to certain destruction because they will do what the Good Samaritan did in the Scriptures."

Perceiving that he made no impression, the shrewd

Captain turned his batteries in another direction. " Consider," he said, " how few we are in numbers, now that Bryant, Reed, Thorn, and Cloutman are gone. Can we afford to lose McLellan, who is one of the strongest and bravest men among us? His wife also can handle a gun as well as most men, and the dog is worth three men at any time. Then there is this boy, as I might call him, if he had not this very day shown the courage and skill of a veteran, — an excellent sharp-shooter, used to the woods, and nearly the only one who dares to go after game, or gets any when he does go, and thus is one great means of our support in these times, when we can raise so little. We may also in a great measure attribute to him the slaughter we have this day made of our enemies."

But the stubborn prejudices in which they had been educated proved too hard for the influence of the Captain, great as it was. Much chagrined and hurt, he said to Hugh, " Myself and Edmund will at least aid you to get them home." Daniel Mosier and Watson also volunteered to go with them. They placed the Indian who was the less wounded upon the horse; Hugh held him on, while William led the animal by the bridle. They carried the other on a blanket stretched across two poles, relieving each other now and then.

When they reached the house, Elizabeth was already there, and had prepared beds for them, and kindled a small fire of pitch-knots to give light, as

they had no candles. She washed their wounds,
which, though many and deep, were flesh wounds,
bound them up, and gave them food. She then
washed the paint from their faces, when she instantly
knew one of them to be the Indian who had brought
her the meat and the skin full of corn when they
were starving. As she looked upon him, their eyes
met. The savage, taking her hand, pressed it upon
his heart, saying, in his broken English, "Squaw
got big heart, — Indian never forget." Then turning to his companion, he said a few words in his
native tongue, upon which the other, also taking her
hand, pressed it to his heart.

She told William, who could speak their language,
to tell them the whole story in respect to the reluctance of the others to admit them to the fort; and
that in the morning they should move out, and come
to live there, and take care of them. She then renewed the fire that they might have light, placed
water where they could reach it in the night, as they
were feverish and thirsty. They then retired and
left them.

Hugh and William still hoed their corn in common with the rest, and were on the best of terms
with them, who, now that the excitement of dispute
was over, felt the silent influence of their example,
and admired that which they could not imitate.
The Indians directed William to gather certain herbs
and barks which they chewed and applied to their
wounds, and which caused them to heal very rapidly,

so that the one that was wounded in the thigh was soon able to go with William to hunt, and to take all the care of the other.

It was upon a Sabbath morning in August, a few months after the removal from the fort, that Hugh came into the house where Elizabeth was catechizing the children, with an expression of great joy upon his features. He sat down by his wife, and, taking her hand in his, said: " Betsy, I have been praying this morning in the woods. I had such views of God, and such a melting of soul, as I never had before. It was uneasy feelings that drove me to my knees. Ever since we left the fort, I have had, at times, great doubts as to whether I did right to expose my family here for the sake of saving the lives of these Indians ; for I have come to know since, that if we had not moved them as we did, a party would have gone out that night, and killed and scalped them, for their scalps would have brought over three hundred dollars. The more I thought of it, so great was the burden of my soul that I knelt down in the woods to cast it on the Lord. As I prayed, it seemed that a heavy weight was lifted from me. I was enabled so to cast myself and my cares upon Him, to feel such sweet confidence and trust in Him, such assurance that I had done right, and that neither I nor mine should ever come to harm by the Indians, that it seemed as though a voice spake to me from above. I mean, therefore, from this time, to dismiss all anxious thoughts from my mind, and endeavor to work and live in trust and confidence in God, and as though it will be as I then felt it would."

Hugh did not suffer his resolve to evaporate in words, for no sooner had he got in his harvest than he began to hew a barn-frame forty feet by thirty-six. As he and his son were busily at work, Captain Phinney came along. "Well," said he, "this is the greatest piece of business I have seen yet. Nobody would think it was war-time, and an Indian war too. But where is the other Indian? There is only one."

"O, he is in the woods, hunting for himself and the rest of us; and a splendid hunter he is too."

"But are you not afraid that, when the other gets well, they will kill you in the night?"

"No."

"But there are other Indians round about. Are you not afraid they will get them to do it?"

"Not a bit of it."

"But is not your wife tired?"

"No," replied Hugh, with a smile, "she don't know what the word means; besides, she believes in Indians. There is no need of their getting up in the night to kill us, for Squid, as we call him, might shoot William at any time, if he liked, for they are often hunting together in the woods."

"Well, I hope it will all turn out well; but I have my fears. How do you know but the Indians will burn your barn?"

" I don't ; but I don't believe they will. In short, Captain, I am like my wife. She says she don't mean to die but once, and that some folks die a hundred times dreading it."

Hugh raised his barn and covered it, and in the winter, after all fears of the Indians were over, went to logging. The Indians, after the other recovered, were taken to Portland to be exchanged, or held as hostages.

The next spring, Hugh determined to plant his corn by himself, and went to work on his land as usual ; and, though Indians were in the neighborhood, they were not molested. Hugh and his family began to suspect that the Indians they had nursed must be among these war-parties, and that they watched over the interests of those who had protected them. For though his cattle ran in the woods, they were not disturbed, while other men lost theirs. This conjecture was soon made certain. Alexander, who had been in the edge of the woods, hunting after a hen's nest, came home out of breath, saying that he had seen Squidrassett; that he was awfully painted ; and that he had told him to run home, for there were Indians round who might carry him off.

A few evenings after this, they were seated round the fire, when the door opened, and in stalked Squidrassett and four other Indians. Hugh and William sprang for their guns ; but Squid told them that they came in peace, and, the more completely to assure

them, took all his comrades' guns and put them out
of doors. Then, pointing to a large, noble-looking
savage, wearing a silver cross and a large breast-
plate, and having his head adorned with eagles'
feathers, his leggings and belt worked with beads and
fringed with deer's hair, and the handle of his knife
inlaid with silver, he told them this was their chief.
Seats were placed for the Indians round the fire;
Elizabeth and the children standing behind, gazing
half in terror, half in wonder, upon the stern coun-
tenances of the Indians in their war-paint.

After a few moments spent in silence, the chief
rose, and thus addressed Hugh: —

"Brother, my young men have told me that it is not
many moons since you came from over the great sea,
and you have never shed the blood of our brothers
the Narragansetts; therefore there are between us
no old wrongs to avenge. They have also told me
that you have never been out on scouting parties for
the scalps of our women and children, to sell them
to your king and sagamores for money. They have
also told us that your son discovered our ambush,
and slew many of our warriors. He has already distinguished himself. He will be a great chief. All
this is right; you were defending your lodges and
your families, and, though you have struck us very
hard, we do not complain. You are brave men,
and we respect you. But there are other things between us.

"When it was peace, and our young men came

Squid makes a Speech.   Page 254.

hungry and tired to your camp, you made them welcome, though you were hungry yourselves; you gave them food, they slept by your fire, and you spread your blanket over them. That was right. It was as the Great Spirit has taught his children, and according to the customs of our fathers. Therefore we call you just.

"But there is another thing, which seems wonderful to us, because neither we nor our old men have ever known anything like it, nor the other tribes, for we have inquired of them. When our people lay in ambush, and you pursued and took them, though you would have done right to kill, or burn them at the stake, you did not. You spake in their behalf, when others wanted to slay them. You likewise came here and took care of them, and in so doing risked your lives. This is what we cannot understand. It is not what Indians would do, and we are sure it is not what white men would do. We often hear white men speak good words, but we never see them do any good things. This is more than brave or just. We therefore think it must be from the Master of Life, who made all things. It has touched our hearts, and therefore we love you and thank you, and have come to tell you that as long as grass grows and water runs there is friendship between you and us, — between your children and our children. If we meet on the war-path, we will strike each other like men. If we slay you when our people meet in battle, we will bury you as though you were of us; if you are wounded, and fall into our hands, we will do to you as you have done to us. We will not kill your cattle, nor burn your lodges, nor hurt anything that is yours. We have also told what you have done to the other tribes, and to the Canada Indians. No Indian will harm you, because we see that you are what we never believed there was, a just white man. I have said. Brother, is it good ? "

Hugh, in reply, expressed his thanks for the kind spirit manifested by the chief, saying he had only acted as he had been taught by the Great Spirit.

" Brother," said the savage, "one word more. This land is ours; the Great Spirit gave it to our fathers. Because the white men are stronger than we, and have taken it from us, it is not therefore theirs. But we now give it to you and to your children, for the good which you have shown to us, and we shall never try to take it from you."

Then the Indian, taking a pipe from his girdle, filled and lighted it, and, having taken a few whiffs, passed it to Hugh and William, and then it went round the circle. Hugh now invited them to eat with him. The repast being finished, the Indians, resuming their arms, departed in Indian file, and were soon lost in the depths of the forest.

William now rose to fasten the door. " Never mind that, Billy," said his father; " we can sleep with open doors after this. The Indians could have killed us all, if they had wished, before we could have pulled a trigger. I shall never go into garrison any more."

CHAPTER XII.

UNCLE BILLY AT HOME.

HUGH was now to reap as he had sown. The noble spirit he had manifested in taking care of the wounded savages brought its own reward. He improved his old fields, and cleared new, while others, confined to the fort for fear of the Indians, let their fields grow up to bushes, and cut scarcely any hay. The gratitude of the Indians had spared his cattle; so he could work his land and haul masts. As England held the empire of the sea, the lumber ships were convoyed, or guarded, by men-of-war, and therefore he continued to lumber and gather stock.

At this period, James and Joseph, sons of Bryce McLellan of Portland, both fell in love with Abigail; but she preferred Joseph. James was a cooper, very plain, but very pious. Joseph was a shipmaster, younger, handsome-built, red-cheeked, of exuberant spirits, as full of mischief and practical jokes as an egg is of meat, but free from vice, enterprising, and, as his after-life proved, knowing how to acquire property. It must be confessed that appearances were against Joseph.

17

Elizabeth considered it to be her duty to select
husbands for her daughters. In so doing, she cared
not a rush for the wealth of the candidate, but was
rather influenced by moral character, and the possession of ability to earn a living. To use her own
definition, " he was the most of a man that had the
property in himself." Elizabeth knew what James
was, — a God-fearing young man, who had a good
trade, and would get a good living, and that was
enough. As for Joseph, he might be very well, —
she hoped he was, — no doubt he was so ; but he was
a sailor, — sailors had great temptations, — they
were rolling stones, and didn't gather much. A
woman who married a sailor had an anxious life.

Joseph and Abigail went blueberrying ; he broke
a gold ring in two, gave half to Abigail, and she hid
it in her bosom. The next day he went to sea.
Elizabeth sent for James to come up. When he
came, she asked her daughter how she liked the man
she had chosen for her husband.

" I don't like him at all, mother," said Abigail ;
" he's old and he's ugly. I won't have him."

" Tell me you won't have the man I have selected
for you ? Which knows best ? You *shall* have
him ; " and she boxed her ears.

Joseph came home, found Abigail married, and
reproached Elizabeth in no measured terms. He
then said, " I'll have Mary ; she is younger, and she
is handsomer."

" You cannot have Mary," was the reply ; " I have
destined her for another man."

"I *will* have her," said Joseph; then, turning to Mary, he asked her on the spot if she would have him, to which she replied in the affirmative.

Grannie Warren always told me (in confidence), when I sat at her knees in the chimney-corner, that Mary, our own grannie, was a true " chip of the old block;" and that her mother, not caring to push matters to extremities with her, made no further opposition.

Abigail had been married in August; and Joseph, determined to make sure work of it this time, was married in September of the same year, 1756. Thus, amid the perils of the Indian war, Hugh and Elizabeth were marrying off their children, and getting property. Hugh even bought such lands as went for a very low price, because of the danger of occupation.

And now had come the 26th of September, 1759. Hugh and his family had just risen, when the quick gallop of a horse driven at full speed was heard; and the next moment the latch was violently pulled up, and in burst Captain Phinney. The Captain's manners were in general very grave and dignified, and he stood much upon ceremony; but on this morning his cocked hat was all awry, his face red with excitement, and his eyes were sparkling.

Catching off his hat, he waved it over the heads of the family, shouting at the top of his voice, "Quebec is captured! Montcalm killed! The

French whipped into shoe-strings! Canada is ours. Bless the Lord! No more Indian wars. Pull down the garrisons, work your farms, go logging, do what you like! God bless his Majesty, King of Great Britain, Scotland, and Ireland, — yes, and Canada! Hurrah!!!"

Out of breath, he sank into a chair, but with a look of inexpressible happiness. The cheer was instantly taken up, and repeated by the whole circle, from Hugh to Martha, the four-year-old.

" Stop and breakfast with us, Captain," said Hugh, after he had heard the news.

" No, I thank you; I am too glad to eat."

" Well, then, let us drink the King's health."

" With all my heart."

It is utterly impossible for us to conceive the extravagant joy which pervaded New England when Canada was conquered. Those who for fourteen years had never labored in their fields, nor sat in the house of God without the musket beside them, nor had ever gone to rest without feeling that they were liable to be waked by the war-whoop, could now rest and pursue their labors undisturbed. Old enmities were forgotten, and men hugged each other in the street for joy. In a few moments the guns of the forts, and of the garrisons all round, and the batteries at Portland, together with the heavier broadsides of the men-of-war in the harbor, were heard celebrating the joyful event.

" It never rains but it pours." The family were

still sitting at the table, being delayed with listening to the good news. Indeed, Hugh was so transported with the tidings, that, for the first time in his life, he didn't care whether he worked or not, when Jane, who was playing before the door, came in crying: " O mother! Uncle Joseph, Uncle James, and Aunt Mary are coming, with a man riding before them what's got women's clothes on, and the funniest cap with two black feathers on it. He's got something under his arm that looks like Uncle Bryce's bellows, with four things sticking over his shoulder; and, mother! he's putting the littlest one in his mouth."

The parents had given attention only to the first portion of Jane's news, as they instantly were engaged in consulting how worthily to entertain their unexpected guests.

" I've enough for breakfast," said Elizabeth.

" I will kill a lamb before dinner; and there are chickens and eggs," said Hugh.

Their deliberations were brought to a close by a shrill sound that with its mighty volume seemed to fill the whole atmosphere.

" It sounds like the buzzing of a thousand swarms of bees," said William.

" There comes the Bumblebee," said Cary, as the strange noise took a deeper tone.

"It's the drone of a bagpipe," cried Hugh, the moment his ear caught the tone, " and it's playing ' Johnnie Cope.' O wife," said he, having by this time reached the door, "it's our own bluid cousin, Archie Campbell, frae Argyle, wi' the pipes, and the kilt, a braw bonnet and plaid, our ain clan colors; and he's blowing away for dear life, God bless him!"

The whole family now rushed bareheaded from the house, and gathered round the guests.

" O Archie!" cried Elizabeth, flinging her arms round his neck the instant his foot was out of the stirrup, and kissing him on both cheeks again and again, — " that I should see my ain kindred, clean frae the braes of Loch Awe, at my ain door." Overcome by her feelings, she lifted up her voice and wept for joy.

No sooner was he released from the grasp of Elizabeth, than Hugh, taking both his hands in his own, said, in a voice that trembled with emotion, " It's a sight for sair e'en to look on your face, my auld companion; mony's the day we have played together, both in Scotland and in Ireland, when we went back and forth to each other's homes, — and how we used to lang for the times to come! But come into the house, all of ye."

" I ken'd ye had not forgotten the auld music o' your native land, and that 'Johnnie Cope' wad bring ye out like a swarm of bees," said Archie. " What a swarm there is of ye, lads and lasses! sae strang and hale looking, not a feckless loon among them, and yourselves looking sae hearty and young. If, as James has been telling me, ye hae seen hard times, it has thriven well with ye. Aweel, ye hae now a

"ARCHIE CAMPBELL FRAE ARGYLE."   Page 262.

house of your own, and can plough your ain land, which ye could never have done at hame."

"But what brought ye here, Archie? You have not told us that."

"I came over with Frazer's Highlanders — but belonged to the 58th — to take Quebec; the transport our company was in was dismasted, and we put into Portland for repairs, and there we heard that the job was done. I got liberty till to-morrow noon, and I stumbled upon James in the street, and he brought me out here."

If ever there was heartfelt satisfaction upon earth, it was to be found that day in that log-house. They had an early supper, and the great fireplace was filled with wood to make the room look cheerful.

"Now, Archie," said Elizabeth, "we hae talked ower auld times, and asked, and ye hae answered, all the questions about the folks at hame that we could think of, though I doubt not we shall think of as many mair when ye are gone. Now get your pipes, and let us have some of the auld songs."

"Weel," replied Archie, "I will begin wi' 'Johnnie Cope,'" and he instantly struck up the familiar tune, the words of which were these: —

> "It was upon an afternoon,
> Sir John marched into Preston town,
> He says, 'My lads, come lean you down,
> And we'll fight the boys in the morning.'
> Hey, Johnnie Cope, are ye wauking yet?
> Or are ye sleeping, I would wit?

O, haste ye, get up, for the drums do beat;
O, fye, Cope, rise in the morning.

"But when he saw the Highland lads,
   Wi' tartan trews, and white cockades,
   Wi' swords and guns, and rungs and gauds,
   O, Johnnie took wings in the morning.
   Hey, Johnnie Cope, &c."

This was succeeded by the "Battle of Killi-crankie," and many others. It is impossible to describe the effect produced upon the minds of his audience by this stormy music, which was connected in their associations with all that the heart holds dear on this side of the grave. The voice of tempests, the roar of a thousand torrents, the memories of many a green valley, and deep, clear lake sleeping among the hills, were recalled by its stirring notes.

As the songs went on, they rose from their seats, clasped each other's hands, and with bending forms kept time to the music; but when Archie played the "Gathering of the Clans," and the very rafters rang to these sounds, that had so often marshalled their kindred to victory or death, and wailed "sav-age and shrill" over so many bloody fields, their eyes filled with tears, and they wept and laughed by turns.

"Good old David danced before the ark," said Elizabeth; "I don't believe he was more rejoiced at the bringing in of the ark than I am at the out-going of this weary war. Gie us a bonny spring, Archie; and I'll see if these waeful years have taken

all the youth out of me." She sprang upon the
floor, and, being joined by Hugh, Joseph, and James,
they did their best to execute a Highland fling.
" There are not enough of us," said she. " If there
were just eight of us Highland folk, wouldn't we
do it now ? "

" Is it not a strange thing," said Archie, stopping
to take breath, " that we Presbyterians of the auld
Kirk, whose fathers fought against the Stuarts, and
took the Solemn League and Covenant, should be so
stirred up by their auld Papistical sangs ? "

" They are our ain country sangs, for a' that they
have been the scout of the heathen," said Hugh.
" A Highlander's heart will leap to the pipes till it
is cold in the grave."

" Did you hear what took place at Quebec ? "

" No."

" The auld fule of a general would not let the
pipes play, and the Highlanders broke, and retreated
in confusion. The Highland officer told the general
he did vera wrang to take the pipes from the Highlanders, that these put life into them, and that even
then they wad be of use. The general said, ' Let
them blow, in God's name, then ! ' The pipers
sounded the charge, and the Highlanders, flinging
off their plaids, rushed upon the French with their
claymores, and drove them before them like sheep."

" Now," said Elizabeth, " that we have had our
nonsense and our songs of bluidshed, let us have
something better. Archie, I know that ye can sing

as well as play ; sing us ' The Battle of the Boyne Water,' — it's good enough to sing in kirk."

Archie accordingly sang the auld song, which, although possessed of no poetical merit, was set to a good old tune, and commemorates a most important event, and the singing of which to-day in most parts of Ireland would expose the singer to a broken head : —

> " July the first, in Oldbridge Town,
>   There was a famous battle,
> Where many men lay on the ground,
>   And cannons loud did rattle.
> King William said, ' I don't deserve
>   The name of Faith's Defender,
> If I don't venture life and limb
>   To make a foe surrender.'
> A bullet from the Irish came,
>   It grazed King William's arm ;
> We thought his Majesty was slain,
>   But it did him little harm.

> " ' Brave boys,' he said, ' be not dismayed,
>   For the loss of one commander ;
> For God will be our king this day,
>   And I'll be general under.'
> Here let us all with heart and hand
>   Unite forever after,
> And bless the glorious memory
>   Of King William who crossed the water."

Hugh was now able to take advantage of the changed condition of the times, and his progress was very rapid. He had a great number of masts on his own lands, and he bought all the land he could get. His great passion was for land; and he acted up to the spirit of Elizabeth's maxim, "We'll risk our scalps for land." They had a fashion of keeping all their property together, and working together, which gave them a great advantage, as it furnished them with capital, and enabled them to undertake larger jobs. "A good many littles make a mickle," said Hugh to his children and relatives, who, with his brother James and his sons-in-law, made quite a numerous company. "We will put it all in one pot, and boil it together, and then we shall have a pot full."

Joseph carried lumber to the West Indies, and they built his vessel, and loaded her from their own forests. They bought timber lands, and on small streams that they could dam with little expense, sawed out their own timber, hauled it with their own teams, and raised their own hay and cattle. Whenever any one married into the family, they all set to work to help him. In short, it was a Highland clan transplanted to the forests of Maine.

"It's time our William was married," said Elizabeth. "He has taken care of everybody else, — he ought to have some happiness himself." She was not one who permitted her resolutions to evaporate in words. She instantly discovered that they had so much spinning to do, that she could not get along without a girl; where she should find a good one, the Lord only knew. At eight of the clock the next morning she was in the saddle with a pillion behind it.

It would seem as if the Lord must have helped Elizabeth ; for at four o'clock in the afternoon she came home, bringing with her a bouncing, corn-fed girl, whom she introduced to the family as Miss Rebecca Huston.   She said it was an excellent family, the Hustons, — good blood, none better, — and they were workers ; that she had never worked out — wouldn't now, only to accommodate a neighbor.

In short, things worked to a charm.   William and Rebecca milked together, and in due time they were married, on June 10, 1765.   William bought a piece of land one mile south of Gorham Corner, — where were the old cellar and orchard to which reference was made in the first chapter.   He added to this by subsequent purchase, till his homestead comprised seven hundred acres covered with a heavy growth of fine timber, and with a stream now called Week's Brook flowing through a portion of it.

It was an occasion of mingled feelings with his parents when William was married.   It was hard parting with him as a member of the household. He was born in the old country, and was a link between them and the home and friends of their youth. His grandparents had seen him, and held him in their arms.   In stature and shape he strongly resembled Hugh's father ; and, as his parents looked upon him, it often brought the tears of old memories to their eyes.   He had also borne the brunt of the battle with them, shoulder to shoulder, during the bitter years of poverty and the deadly perils of the

Indian war. Then, too, he had been most trustworthy, even from boyhood, — if it could be said that he ever had any boyhood ; he had settled all the disputes of the younger children, and kept all around him in good-humor.

There was at that time no road from Gorham to Scarborough. William, his father, and his brothers, went into the dense forest, cleared a square of three acres, hauled out what timber they wanted for building, and burned the rest and planted the ground with corn. In the midst of this he put up his house and barn, September 15, 1763. As soon as one room was finished, he moved in. So thick was the forest at that time, and so completely was he buried in the woods, that he unyoked his oxen, and drove them in loose through the trees, rolled in the wheels of his cart, and carried the tongue and axletree on his shoulder.

He began housekeeping with himself and wife and four joiners, probably the smallest family he ever had, although without children of his own. He always liked to have many at the table and many at the fireside ; and the last thing before he went to bed, it was his custom to go out and look around to see if there was any benighted traveller in sight.

The year after his house was built, a road was cleared directly by it to Scarborough, and people began to haul lumber. He then placed a seat between two trees that stood beside the road for wayfarers and the teamsters, who always stopped to water their cattle at the hill, to rest upon. If half a dozen came along at dinner-time, they were always asked to eat. His wife was just like him in this respect; if he liked to provide, she liked just as well to cook. She was as droll and keen of wit as her husband, and it was impossible to spend an evening there without many a hearty laugh.

The first meal they sat down to in their new house was supper. William provided abundantly, and charged his wife to fill both ovens.

" Why, William," replied she, "there are but six of us, and here is enough for twenty."

" Well, so there ought to be; this is the first meal in our new house, the first meal's victuals you ever cooked as my wife. Mother says you must have *lashings* the first meal, for just as sure as you have a little ' scrimped-up' mess, you will have it so all your life; but if you begin with enough, you will always have enough, and she knows. Perhaps, too, somebody may come in before we get through."

" I am sure I don't know where they should come from, except we invite in the crows, — we are not so near to neighbors; but if a dozen should come, there is enough."

They had scarcely begun to eat when there was a knock at the door. " Come in!" shouted William. A singular-looking man made his appearance, in the remnants of a tattered uniform, who, after making a military salute, exclaimed, " God save all here!"

" Good-day, friend; God's blessing hurts no man,"

said William. " Sit ye down and eat with us,"
kicking a chair to the table with his foot, while Rebecca laid a plate. " Now, friend," said William,
waving his hand over the table, " there are the victuals, and there " (pointing to the knife and fork)
" are the tools; fall to, and show yourself a ' work-
man that needeth not to be ashamed.' It is just as
free as water."

The meal being over, they drew together round
the fire. Uncle Billy — as we shall now call him,
as he had plenty of nephews and nieces, — besides,
everybody loved him and called him so — then said
to his guest, " What may be your name, friend? and
whence do you come ? "

" My name is Andrew McCulloch," said the
stranger; " they call me Sandie for short. I'll never
deny my country : I am Scotch born and bred."

" Scotland is a country no one need be ashamed
of," replied Uncle Billy, " though she has good reason to be ashamed of many of her children."

" I'm thinking ye may come from Scotland yourself."

" From Ireland last, but our forbears were from
Argyle. Have you been long in the Colonies ? "

" Only three months; but I have been long from
home, in all parts of the world. I have been a soldier."

" And have deserted ? " said Uncle Billy.

Sandie made a gesture of assent.

" What will you do, and where will you put your

head this winter, Sandie ? " inquired his host. " If
you fall into the hands of the king's officers you'll
be shot."

" That is more than I know," replied Sandie.

" Can you chop, or hoe, or mow, or drive oxen ? "

" No ; but I suppose I might learn."

" And who's going to keep you and feed you,
while you are of little or no use, and are learning ? "

" I don't know ; but I know one thing, and that
is, I have suffered misery enough coming through
the woods from Canada. I have been almost starved
to death, and I don't know why it was that I, who
have taken so many other people's lives, did not end
my misery by taking my own." His eyes filled at
the recollection of his sufferings.

" Well, Sandie," said Uncle Billy, " you'll be safer
here in the forest than anywhere else. In the short
days that are coming, you will be worth no more
than your board and your tobacco, — which an old
soldier can't live without, I suppose, — nor all of
that, indeed. If you like to stay here, and mind
the house and the barn, while I am in the woods,
you can just stop where you are; you'll be learning
something to keep yourself with. In the spring,
when the birds are singing and the travelling is
good, you can take up your march, or, if you are
agreeable then, I will give you wages. I keep all
that will work, none that won't ; but any way you
will stop the night with us, and break your fast in
the morning. It's my custom, and that of all our

kin, to suffer no one to go away from the door hungry, — it would bring a curse on the roof-tree."

"May the good God, who guided me here, bless you!" said Sandie, quite overcome, in the fulness of his heart. "Surely, what I lack in knowledge I'll make up in good-will;" and then, with the levity pertaining to a soldier, he put away all his troubles, and, taking "heart of grace," sang songs, told stories, and cracked jokes that made Uncle Billy laugh till he cried.

"I'm glad we've got somebody in the house," said Uncle Billy, looking complacently upon the company; "it isn't natural to me to live with only the wife and cat."

The old adage was abundantly verified in Uncle Billy's case: as he began housekeeping with a feast, so had he plenty all the way through. As he began with welcoming the wayfarer, so was he never without a retinue to eat his cheer, and warm themselves at his hearth. He fed every poor creature, and then set them to work.

There was good fruit in Cambridge, even at that day. When Uncle Billy was there, in Washington's army, he saved the seeds of all the apples he ate, and when he came home planted them, and lived to eat the fruit. The seeds, planted in the new soil, full of ashes, grew rapidly, and bear fruit still. That is where the old orchard came from.

Among his domestics, in later days, were two original characters, Thomas Gustin and Mary Green.

18

Tom was good-natured and lazy, — that is, as lazy as anybody could be where Uncle Billy was, — and a great eater. Mary was a good drudge, but had a long tongue, and would say what she had a mind to. Aunt 'Becca bought a cap that was of fashionable shape, and being excessively proud of it, wore it a while every day to show it. Mary got one just like it, and putting it on, sailed into the front room and sat down beside her mistress. The old lady took off her own cap, flung it on the floor, and set her feet upon it. At this Mary exploded. "Madam McLellan!" said she, "I'd have you to know that the Almighty made me as well as you, that he made us both out of the same clay, and that I have just as good a right to wear a nice cap in His sight as you have."

"Yes, Mary," replied Aunt 'Becca; "he did indeed make us out of the same clay, and out of the same clay the potter hath power to make a slop-jar or a china bowl."

Nothing could confuse Uncle Billy, nor could any accident prevent him from accomplishing his purpose. Sandie used to say, "You might as well draw a blister on Owen Runnel's wooden leg as to outwit Uncle Billy, for he could 'put a keel into a fly.'" For example, when they came to haul the big mast on the stump of which they turned the yoke of cattle, the strongest and best yoke of oxen they had split their yoke. The company supposed they must go home, and give it up for the day

Uncle Billy said, "No, it would never do for so many men and cattle to break off and go home." He guessed he could fix it.

"Fix it, Mr. McLellan!" said Daniel Mosier; "it's split from end to end."

They had no other tool than an axe. He cut down a straight-grained rock-maple, cut off it the proper length, and fitted it to the oxen's necks with the axe and a jack-knife. He then split it in two parts, and cut holes in each part to receive the bows, fastened the two parts together with beech withes, and drew wedges under them, chained the ring on, and wedged that, and then hauled the mast.

Uncle Billy's homestead consisted of a large two-story house, set endwise to the road, facing south, with a barn a hundred feet long, connected with the house by a shed of the same length. At the northeast end was a row of Lombardy poplars. The approach to the front was by a lane, and the front windows permitted a view of the orchard, at the western end of which was a row of cherry-trees. Here the good man lived, making all round him happy, and "the blessing of him that was ready to perish came upon him." Here, too, he died, many years later, by decay of nature, at the age of eighty-one.

They owned in the family fifteen hundred acres of land, covered with a heavy growth of timber, and were in possession of large stocks of cattle and mills. Hugh paid the largest tax of any one in the town, and still lived in the old log-house. It was on a Thanksgiving, and the children were assembled at their father's table. "Mother," said William, "your family is too big for your house. If you have any more grandchildren, you must have a larger house, or we must eat Thanksgiving out of doors. Boys, what do you say to building the old folks a better house? If they won't take care of themselves, we must take care of them."

His words fell on willing ears, and were like sparks upon tow. "A house for father and mother!" was the unanimous cry.

"Well, my children," replied Hugh, his eyes glistening at this evidence of affection, "your mother and I have sometimes talked over the matter, but we have hated to leave the old spot, where we have had so many good and bad times, and where God has blessed us; besides, we always thought more of your comfort than of our own. We came to this country that our children might be better off than ourselves. Your mother has always said, when we have talked about it, that as we both belong to a race that had lands and lived in their stone houses, and as they turned her out of doors for marrying a poor man, and we now have more land than any of them, if she has a house, it shall be a brick one."

"I might as well out with it at once," said Elizabeth. "I should like to let my uncle that spit upon me, and trampled me under foot, and my dainty cousins who used to come down to the brook where I was bleaching linen, tossing their heads, and jeering, and pointing me out to the midshipmen and the young officers of the army that waited on them as their cousin who made a fool of herself, and married below her degree, with a *mechanic*, — though all they could bring against him was that he had neither their pride, their laziness, nor their vices, — I say I should like to let them know that the poor mechanic owns more land than ever they did, lives in a brick house, and is the bonniest Highland laddie that ever a lass was wedded to ; " — and, sitting down in his lap, she put her arms round his neck, and gave him a hearty kiss. " Then," continued she, " I 'll write a letter to Ireland to my old gossip, Sandie Wilson, who's carried many a love-token between your father and me, and ask him to let them know it ; and he will take no small pleasure in doing the errand."

" That's right, mother," said Alexander ; " I glory in your spunk."

" Well, boys," said Hugh, " you must not think that your mother and I are going to spend all that we have earned so hardly to live in a brick house. I would rather live in the old camp. If we do it, we must do it within ourselves, as we have done everything else ; then there'll be no ' after-clap.' "

" I don't see how we can do much of it ourselves," said William ; " we are not masons."

" We can make the bricks, and hew all the timber, make the shingles, saw all the boards at our own mills, burn the bricks with our own wood, pay Jonathan Bryant for the mason-work in a great measure off the farm, and indeed do every part of it, except making and burning the bricks, at odd jobs after haying and harvest; and if we are ten years building it, it will be ours, and paid for when it is done. When I was a lad, I worked a spell with my Uncle Robert, who was a brickmaker. I can make the mill, mould the bricks, temper the clay, and set up the kiln. I may have to get some one to show me about building the arches, but that will not be much. I call that doing it pretty much within ourselves."

They were four years in building the house; but they built it as Hugh and his children did everything they set their hands to, and they did it well. The old timbers, with the axe-clips of Hugh and William, are sound to this day, and the walls as firm as ever. A brick in the wall marked by the fingers of Elizabeth records the date of its erection; and the spring from which they drank, and from which William drew water the night before the slaughter of the Bryants, while the Indians ambushed the path, one hundred and twenty-one years ago, still slakes the traveller's thirst.

Hugh, after having gained the victory in life's struggles, and lived to see his adopted land a free republic and his sons partakers in the conflict, died at the ripe age of seventy-seven, having seen the church of which he was a ruling elder, and with

which he began to worship in a log meeting-house
with the rifle between his knees, increasing and
firmly established.

Thomas, the youngest son, inherited the homestead; and with him Elizabeth lived, still retaining
her energy of character and unbounded hospitality.
During the Revolutionary war, Hugh and Thomas
being from home, three men came to the door, and
wanted to stay through the night. Her son's wife
was frightened, and refused to receive them. Elizabeth, now an aged woman, heard the conversation,
and came to the door. "Where are you from,
friends?"

"We are soldiers from Washington's army, going
home. The Continental money is good for nothing,
and we are begging our way."

"Come into the house, and may God bless you!
My sons are soldiers. No men who have fought
under Washington will harm a lone woman like
me."

She took them to her own room, gave them a
warm meal, made them up a good bed on the floor,
and slept herself in the same room, lying down with
her clothes on, as her daughter-in-law, Jenny, was
afraid to have them in her part of the house. In
the morning she got them breakfast, and filled their
haversacks with provisions.

After Jenny came into the family, she wished to
have things a little more in conformity with modern
usage. They had a slave by the name of Philipps,

old and almost blind. They kept the **cream-pot** in winter in the oven, to keep it from freezing. Philipps used to get up in the night, take the cream, and make cream-porridge. Jenny declared she wouldn't put up with such doings. Philipps persevered. She appealed to Elizabeth, who refused to interfere, saying it was misery enough to be a poor old negro, and blind to boot. " Let him have his cream, there is plenty of it.'' Elizabeth was not made up to order, she was one of nature's nobility ; she cherished other feelings in respect to the old slave than those of the younger woman. He was an old, faithful servant, had carried on his shoulders the bricks and mortar to build the mansion, and she felt that he deserved consideration at her hands in his decrepitude. But Jenny determined to put a stop to it. She took the cream-pot out of the oven, and set in its place the blue-dye pot, with its unsavory contents. The blind negro went to the oven the next night, poured out a quart of blue dye into the kettle, and made his porridge. The next morning everything in the kitchen was spattered with blue dye that he had sputtered out; and when Thomas came into the room, Philipps greeted him with, " Massa Thomas, what for you bring that wretch here? Send her back where she came from."

Elizabeth lived to the great age of ninety-six years, leaving at her death two hundred and thirty-four living descendants.